DEDICATION

I would like to dedicate this book to the following: My wife, Emilee, who has been selfless throughout this process; she's a great partner and advisor; thank you for your love, guidance, and belief in me. My daughter, Quinn, who makes every day great; the Bengals are already a big part of her life, and she went on her first road trip when she was just a few weeks old. My parents, Barb and Glenn, who taught me at a young age that I could accomplish my goals in life with hard work and dedication. Everyone who has guided and helped me reach this point; there are countless people who have given me advice or helped me professionally over the years—thank you. This book is a culmination of a lot of hard work, some luck, and having plenty of great people around me.

Edited by Ryan Jacobson. Proofread by Emily Beaumont. Fact-checked by Natalie Fowler. Cover logo by Madhusanka. Background garnish by Y. Shane Nitzsche. Interior design by Ryan Jacobson and Y. Shane Nitzsche

Joe Burrow photograph (front cover) by Joe Robbins. Copyright 2023 The Associated Press. Football photograph (back cover) by Billion Photos/Shutterstock.com. Football helmet (spine) by RazorGraphix/Shutterstock.com. For additional photography credits, see page 150.

10 9 8 7 6 5 4 3 2 1

Copyright 2023 by James Rapien
Published by Lake 7 Creative, LLC
Minneapolis, MN 55412
www.lake7creative.com

ISBN: 978-1-940647-99-9

FOOTBALL ABBREVIATIONS

AFC: American Football Conference

AFL: American Football League

C: Center

CB: Cornerback

CFL: Canadian Football League

DB: Defensive back

DE: Defensive end

DT: Defensive tackle

FL: Flanker

FS: Free safety

FB: Fullback

G: Guard

HB: Halfback

K: Kicker

KR: Kick returner

LB: Linebacker

LE: Left end

LG: Left guard

LH: Left halfback

LS: Long snapper

LT: Left tackle

MLB: Middle linebacker

MVP: Most valuable player

NFC: National Football Conference

NFL: National Football League

NT: Nose tackle

OLB: Outside linebacker

OT: Offensive tackle / Overtime

P: Punter

PR: Punt returner

QB: Quarterback

RB: Running back

RE: Right end

RG: Right guard

RH: Right halfback

RT: Right tackle

T: Tackle

TE: Tight end

S: Safety

SS: Strong safety

ST: Special teams

UDFA: Undrafted free agent

USFL: United States Football League

WR: Wide receiver

FOREWORD

One of the most enjoyable things about being the Bengals' radio play-by-play voice is having breakfast with team president Mike Brown and my broadcast partner Dave Lapham. It's a tradition on the morning of every road game. At exactly 7 a.m. in a banquet room at the team hotel, I join Mike, his close friend Jack Schiff, Lap, and frequently team executives Katie and Troy Blackburn for an hour of gut-busting laughter as Mike and Lap share stories from their remarkable football lives.

On a typical morning, the topics might include a description of Paul Brown sternly critiquing a panic-stricken rookie in front of his teammates, former Bengals who comically struggled to deal with crowd noise, and Lap's strength-building days as a 14-year-old moving company "lugger."

In addition to the laughs, I also get valuable history lessons about the Cincinnati Bengals and the many great players and coaches who have thrilled and entertained us for more than 50 years.

While the Bengals have come up just short in their quest to win a Super Bowl title, the team has had an extraordinary impact on the National Football League (NFL), beginning with the most innovative coach in sports history: team founder Paul Brown.

"There's nobody in the game that I have more respect for than Paul Brown," said six-time Super Bowl-winning head coach Bill Belichick. "His contributions to the game, to the way it's played, to protective equipment, to the playbook; every film breakdown, every meeting, and everything that he did as a coach, 50 years later everybody is still basically doing the same thing. I really think of him as the father of professional football."

The cutting-edge approach continued under Brown's disciples, as Sam Wyche, Bill Walsh, and Dick LeBeau helped invent the no-huddle attack, the West Coast offense (more accurately the Ohio River offense), and the Zone Blitz defense.

And the standout players who have proudly worn the orange and black include the greatest offensive lineman in NFL history in Anthony Munoz; a pair of MVP quarterbacks in Ken Anderson and Boomer Esiason; ferocious defensive standouts like Tim Krumrie, David Fulcher, and Geno Atkins; colorful personalities like Cris Collinsworth, Chad Johnson, and Ickey Woods; and consummate pros like Ken Riley, Isaac Curtis, and A.J. Green.

Not to mention the current stars led by Joe Burrow and Ja'Marr Chase.

The unforgettable moments in Bengals history include three trips to the Super Bowl, Corey Dillon's 278-yard rushing performance, Burrow's 525-yard passing day, "You don't live in Cleveland," the "Fumble in the Jungle," and, of course, the "Freezer Bowl."

I was thrilled when my friend James Rapien informed me that he was working on *Enter the Jungle*. A coffee-table book about the Cincinnati Bengals with vivid color photographs and a comprehensive look at the team's legendary players and monumental victories is long overdue.

As a writer, podcaster, and reporter, James has quickly become an important source of information for Cincinnati fans. He covers the team with a critical eye but also displays the passion of a lifelong fan. His zeal for all things Bengals is abundantly clear in this book.

I know that Bengals fans are going to love *Enter the Jungle*. Who knows? I might bring it up one morning at breakfast with Mike and Lap.

—Dan Hoard
Voice of the Bengals

TABLE OF CONTENTS

A Bit of NFL History 7

Author's Notes 7

Introduction 8

1968 10

1969 12

1970 14

Paul Brown 17

1971 18

1972 20

1973 22

1974 24

1975 26

1976 28

Ken Anderson 31

1977 32

1978 34

1979 36

All-1970s Team 38

1980 40

1981 42

Super Season 44

1982 46

1983 48

1984 50

1985 52

1986 54

1987 56

1988 58

A Game for the Ages 61

1989 62

All-1980s Team 64

1990 66

1991 68

1992 70

1993 72

1994 74

1995 76

1996 78

1997 80

Hall-of-Famers 82

1998 84

1999 86

All-1990s Team 88

2000 90

Dillon Runs Wild 92

2001 94

2002 96

2003 98

2004 100

2005 102

Playoffs, at Last 104

2006 106

2007 108

2008 110

2009 112

All-2000s Team 114

2010 116

2011 118

Best Catches 121

2012 122

2013 124

2014 126

2015 128

2016 130

2017 132

Marvin Lewis 135

2018 136

2019 138

All-2010s Team 140

2020 142

2021 144

AFC Champions 146

2022 148

Photo Credits 150

Sources 151

About the Author 152

A BIT OF NFL HISTORY

The Cincinnati Bengals joined the American Football League (AFL) in 1968. The Denver Broncos, Kansas City Chiefs, Oakland Raiders, and San Diego Chargers were the other four teams in the AFL West Division.

The AFL merged with the National Football League (NFL) in 1970. Bengals owner Paul Brown pushed for the merger. Cincinnati joined a four-team American Football Conference (AFC) Central Division that included the Cleveland Browns, Houston Oilers, and Pittsburgh Steelers. The Jacksonville Jaguars were founded in 1995 and joined the AFC Central. In 1996, the Cleveland Browns became the Baltimore Ravens. However, the Browns started again as a new franchise in 1999, making the AFC Central a six-team division. Meanwhile, the Houston Oilers became the Tennessee Oilers in 1997, then the Tennessee Titans in 1999. The NFL realigned its divisions in 2002. The Bengals, Browns, Ravens, and Steelers moved into the AFC North.

From 1968 to 1977, the Bengals played a 14-game regular-season schedule. That became 16 games per season in 1978. Labor disputes between the Players Association and the league prevented teams from playing their full schedules in 1982 and 1987, when they played 9 and 15 games, respectively. The NFL expanded to a 17-game regular-season schedule in 2021.

AUTHOR'S NOTES

Pro Bowl: All Pro Bowl selections include original ballot picks as recognized by the Cincinnati Bengals Official Media Guide. AFL All-Stars are designated as Pro Bowl selections.

Key Additions: A big part of telling the story of the Cincinnati Bengals comes from acknowledging the most influential players that the team added on an annual basis. The selections are subjective. They're based on impact, length of tenure, and achievements with the organization.

Sacks: The NFL did not make sacks an official statistic until 1982. Any sack numbers referenced before 1982 are courtesy of Pro Football Reference.

Starting Lineups: Starting lineups change weekly due to injuries, rotations, and the opponent. With that in mind, the players listed are recognized as the primary starters for that season according to the Cincinnati Bengals Media Guide. While I did my best, the alignments may not be perfect. (For example, wide receivers might not be on their most typical sides of the field.) However, the starting lineups should give you a good idea of which players had the biggest impacts at their respective positions.

INTRODUCTION

To some, the Cincinnati Bengals are simply one of 32 NFL teams—but for a young Cincinnati native like myself, they were much more than that. When I was growing up, watching or listening to games became part of my Sunday routine. My family wasn't big into sports, but they quickly realized I was going to change that. I couldn't get enough of the Bengals—even though I fell in love with them during their worst decade in franchise history: the 1990s.

If you want to learn more about the franchise that Paul Brown founded in 1968, this book is for you. It's designed for fans of all ages. From the early days, when Brown successfully guided the Bengals from the American Football League (AFL) to the National Football League (NFL), to the glory years of the 1980s, when Cincinnati danced the "Ickey Shuffle" and the team fell just short of their first world championship, the highs and the lows of the organization are captured here.

The first chapter of the Bengals' history began following the 1962 NFL season. Brown, who had been the head coach and general manager of the Cleveland Browns, was fired by owner Art Modell. A few years later, Brown's son Mike helped identify Cincinnati as a potential location for a new team. Cincinnati was awarded an AFL expansion franchise on May 24, 1967. The league approved an ownership group led by Brown a few months later.

Brown looked to the past for his new team's nickname. From 1937 to 1941, Cincinnati had been home to a professional football team called the "Bengals." It became an obvious choice for the nickname of this new franchise.

The team played their first game on Friday, September 6, 1968: a 29–13 loss to the San Diego Chargers. Nine days later, on September 15, the Bengals earned their first win, 24–10, over the Denver Broncos.

The Bengals spent two seasons in the AFL before transitioning to the NFL in 1970. There, Cincinnati became one of 26 teams in the newly combined league. They were joined by the Cleveland Browns, Houston Oilers, and Pittsburgh Steelers in the American Football Conference (AFC) Central Division.

As of the end of the 2022 NFL season, the Bengals have won 12 division titles and three AFC championships. They have made three Super Bowl appearances in 55 years of existence. The team has had some memorably bad seasons, but they consistently won division titles and qualified for the playoffs in the 1970s and 1980s. After an ugly stretch that lasted for most of the 1990s, the Bengals rebounded to eventually field a winner after hiring Marvin Lewis as their head coach and after taking quarterback Carson Palmer with the first pick in the 2003 NFL Draft.

There's something special about Cincinnati's love for the Bengals. Even during lean years, our passionate fans continue to cherish and support the team. And during those seasons in which the Bengals are competitive? The city takes its passion to another level. You can't go anywhere without seeing orange and black.

Yes, Bengals fans are the best for a multitude of reasons, and that's why this book means so much to me. *Enter the Jungle* can be a guide for all fans—young and old. You'll learn about the franchise that we love so much: from how it was founded to key moments in its history. There are the historic runs to the Super Bowl. There's Corey Dillon breaking Walter Payton's single-game rushing record (and snapping a 0–6 start to the 2000 season). Coincidentally, that was one of the handful of Bengals games I attended as a child. It was absolutely electric. Being in the stands for that moment is something I'll always remember.

I also attended a few games at Cinergy Field before Paul Brown Stadium was completed in 2000. Long before then, as some fans may not know, while Riverfront Stadium was being built, the Bengals played their 1968 and 1969 home games at Nippert Stadium on the University of Cincinnati campus.

Let this book be your tour through the Bengals' history. Learn about the peaks and valleys, and embrace the journey. This franchise hasn't yet won the ultimate prize, but we've gotten close—and made plenty of memories along the way. Learning the history of this team will make the moment that much sweeter when we do win a Lombardi Trophy.

The Bengals are such a big part of the Cincinnati area and the day-to-day lives of so many fans—not just in Cincinnati but across the country. *Enter the Jungle* is for every person who roots for the team and for every person who wants to learn more about a franchise that has grown so much since its inception in 1968.

Enjoy this book as we walk through time and look back at the history of the Cincinnati Bengals.

—James Rapien

3–11
Fifth in AFL West

The Cincinnati Bengals played their home games at Nippert Stadium on the University of Cincinnati's campus in 1968. A new two-sport stadium was being built in downtown Cincinnati that both the Bengals and Major League Baseball's Cincinnati Reds would call home.

The Bengals' inaugural season started with a loss in San Diego, but the team quickly rebounded with double-digit wins over the Denver Broncos and Buffalo Bills at home.

Unfortunately for the Bengals, a 2–1 start proved to be the high point of their first season. The team lost seven straight games and 10 of their final 11 contests to finish the year in last place in the AFL West.

Paul Brown, legendary former head coach of the NFL's Cleveland Browns, led the ownership group that founded the Bengals, and Brown also served as the team's head coach.

He started three different quarterbacks during the 1968 campaign: John Stofa, Dewey Warren, and Sam Wyche. (Wyche would go on to become the Bengals' head coach from 1984 to 1991 and would lead Cincinnati to an appearance in Super Bowl XXIII.)

Rookie running back Paul Robinson was a bright spot for the team, leading the AFL in rushing with 1,023 yards. He also scored eight touchdowns and was named the AFL Rookie of the Year.

Tight end Bob Trumpy led the team in receiving, hauling in 37 receptions for 639 yards and three touchdowns. Center Bob Johnson was the Bengals' first draft pick in team history.

Pro Bowl Selections

- Bob Johnson (C)
- Paul Robinson (RB)
- Bob Trumpy (TE)

Schedule

	OPPONENT	SCORE	RECORD
L	@ San Diego Chargers	13–29	0–1
W	Denver Broncos	24–10	1–1
W	Buffalo Bills	34–23	2–1
L	San Diego Chargers	10–31	2–2
L	@ Denver Broncos	7–10	2–3
L	@ Kansas City Chiefs	3–13	2–4
L	Miami Dolphins	22–24	2–5
L	@ Oakland Raiders	10–31	2–6
L	Houston Oilers	17–27	2–7
L	Kansas City Chiefs	9–16	2–8
W	@ Miami Dolphins	38–21	3–8
L	Oakland Raiders	0–34	3–9
L	@ Boston Patriots	14–33	3–10
L	@ New York Jets	14–27	3–11

Season Leaders

CATEGORY	TOTAL	PLAYER
Passing Yards	896	John Stofa
Rushing Yards	1,023	Paul Robinson
Receiving Yards	639	Bob Trumpy
Receptions	37	Bob Trumpy
Interceptions	3	Jess Phillips
Sacks	9	Andy Rice
Points	59	Dale Livingston

Key Additions:
Al Beauchamp (draft), Howard Fest (draft), Bob Johnson (draft), Essex Johnson (draft), Pat Matson (expansion draft), Jess Phillips (draft), Paul Robinson (draft), Bob Trumpy (draft)

Bob Johnson (54) was the second-overall pick in the 1968 AFL Draft.

Starting Lineup

OFFENSE	POSITION
John Stofa	QB
Paul Robinson	RB
Tommie Smiley	RB
Rod Sherman	WR
Warren McVea	WR
Bob Trumpy	TE
Ernie Wright	LT
Dave Middendorf	LG
Bob Johnson	C
Pat Matson	RG
Howard Fest	RT

DEFENSE	POSITION
Jim Griffin	DE
Andy Rice	DT
Bill Staley	DT
Harry Gunner	DE
Al Beauchamp	OLB
Sherrill Headrick	MLB
Frank Buncom	OLB
Fletcher Smith	CB
Charlie King	CB
Jess Phillips	SS
Bobby Hunt	FS

SPECIAL TEAMS	POSITION
Dale Livingston	K
Essex Johnson/ Warren McVea	KR
Dale Livingston	P
Essex Johnson	PR

1969

4-9-1
Fifth in AFL West

The Bengals selected quarterback Greg Cook with the fifth pick in the 1969 AFL Draft. Cook led the Bengals to a 3–0 start, throwing for 581 yards and six touchdowns in the process. The rookie appeared destined for stardom, but he would instead go down as perhaps the biggest "What If?" in team history.

Unfortunately, Cook suffered a shoulder injury in a Week 3 win over the Kansas City Chiefs. He managed to start eight more games throughout the season, but the damage had been done.

Cook showed flashes of his potential, such as his performance against Houston in Week 9, throwing for 298 yards and four touchdowns. Yet he only managed 20 yards passing in Week 5 against the New York Jets and only attempted three passes in Week 12 against the Buffalo Bills.

The Bengals lost four straight games after Cook's injury. They also lost five straight games to end the season.

Despite the inconsistent play, Cook was named AFL Offensive Rookie of the Year. He averaged 9.4 yards per attempt, which remains a Bengals record. Leading receivers Eric Crabtree (21.4) and Bob Trumpy (22.6) averaged over 21 yards per reception, which shows how gifted of a passer Cook truly was.

Owner/coach Paul Brown thought he had drafted the next great star quarterback. Instead, an unfortunate shoulder injury and multiple surgeries derailed Cook's career. He would only play in one more game after 1969: an appearance in Week 1 of the 1973 season, during which he completed one of three passes for 11 yards.

The Bengals picked linebacker Bill Bergey in the second round (31st overall) of the 1969 AFL Draft. He was named AFL Defensive Rookie of the Year.

Pro Bowl Selections

- Bill Bergey (LB)
- Paul Robinson (RB)
- Bob Trumpy (TE)

Schedule

	OPPONENT	SCORE	RECORD
W	Miami Dolphins	27–21	1–0
W	San Diego Chargers	34–20	2–0
W	Kansas City Chiefs	24–19	3–0
L	@ San Diego Chargers	14–21	3–1
L	New York Jets	7–21	3–2
L	Denver Broncos	23–30	3–3
L	@ Kansas City Chiefs	22–42	3–4
W	Oakland Raiders	31–17	4–4
T	@ Houston Oilers	31–31	4–4–1
L	Boston Patriots	14–25	4–5–1
L	@ New York Jets	7–40	4–6–1
L	@ Buffalo Bills	13–16	4–7–1
L	@ Oakland Raiders	17–37	4–8–1
L	@ Denver Broncos	16–27	4–9–1

Season Leaders

CATEGORY	TOTAL	PLAYER
Passing Yards	1,854	Greg Cook
Rushing Yards	578	Jess Phillips
Receiving Yards	855	Eric Crabtree
Receptions	40	Eric Crabtree
Interceptions	4	Four players tied
Sacks	6	Andy Rice
Points	80	Horst Muhlmann

Key Additions:
Bill Bergey (draft), Royce Berry (draft), Greg Cook (draft), Horst Muhlmann (free agent), Ken Riley (draft)

Starting Lineup

OFFENSE	POSITION
Greg Cook	QB
Jess Phillips	RB
Paul Robinson	RB
Eric Crabtree	WR
Speedy Thomas	WR
Bob Trumpy	TE
Ernie Wright	LT
Ernie Park	LG
Bob Johnson	C
Guy Dennis	RG
Howard Fest	RT

DEFENSE	POSITION
Royce Berry	DE
Andy Rice	DT
Bill Staley	DT
Steve Chomyszak	DE
Al Beauchamp	OLB
Bill Bergey	MLB
Bill Peterson	OLB
Fletcher Smith	CB
Ken Riley	CB
Al Coleman	SS
Bobby Hunt	FS

SPECIAL TEAMS	POSITION
Horst Muhlmann	K
Essex Johnson	KR
Dale Livingston	P
Essex Johnson	PR

Greg Cook was named one of the team's 50 greatest players, despite playing in just 12 career games.

"Football is a game of errors. The team that makes the fewest errors in a game usually wins."
—Paul Brown

8–6
First in AFC Central

The Bengals joined the National Football League (NFL) in 1970 due to the AFL-NFL merger. Owner/coach Paul Brown was intent on getting back into the NFL after being fired by Browns owner Art Modell in 1963. The two leagues became one: a 26-team league divided into two 13-team conferences.

Three NFL teams—the Baltimore Colts, Cleveland Browns, and Pittsburgh Steelers—joined the 10 AFL teams to become the American Football Conference (AFC). The Bengals, Browns, Steelers, and Houston Oilers comprised the new four-team AFC Central Division.

Cincinnati won their first-ever NFL game, defeating the Oakland Raiders. They followed that by losing six straight games. The 1–6 start was far from ideal, especially after winning just seven combined games in their first two years as a franchise. But that's when the AFL-NFL merger became a magical season for the Bengals.

They turned things around over the final seven games, beginning with a blowout win in Buffalo, 43–14. Cincinnati won seven straight contests, which included victories over all three of their AFC Central rivals. The streak was capped with a 45–7 win over the Boston Patriots in Week 14. The Bengals won the AFC Central Division and were playoff bound for the first time in franchise history.

Unfortunately, the Bengals' run came to an end at the hands of quarterback Johnny Unitas, who led the Colts to a 17–0 win in the playoffs.

Despite the loss, Cincinnati's first season in the NFL was successful. Brown got some sweet revenge on the team that had cast him aside nearly a decade earlier: The Cleveland Browns finished one win behind the Bengals and didn't qualify for the playoffs.

Pro Bowl Selections

- Lemar Parrish (CB)
- Bob Trumpy (TE)

Schedule

OPPONENT		SCORE	RECORD
W	Oakland Raiders	31–21	1–0
L	@ Detroit Lions	3–38	1–1
L	Houston Oilers	13–20	1–2
L	@ Cleveland Browns	27–30	1–3
L	Kansas City Chiefs	19–27	1–4
L	@ Washington	0–20	1–5
L	@ Pittsburgh Steelers	10–21	1–6
W	@ Buffalo Bills	43–14	2–6
W	Cleveland Browns	14–10	3–6
W	Pittsburgh Steelers	34–7	4–6
W	New Orleans Saints	26–6	5–6
W	@ San Diego Chargers	17–14	6–6
W	@ Houston Oilers	30–20	7–6
W	Boston Patriots	45–7	8–6
L	@ *Baltimore Colts*	*0–17*	*0–1*

Season Leaders

CATEGORY	TOTAL	PLAYER
Passing Yards	1,647	Virgil Carter
Rushing Yards	648	Jess Phillips
Receiving Yards	542	Chip Myers
Receptions	32	Chip Myers
Interceptions	5	Lemar Parrish
Sacks	7.5	Steve Chomyszak
Points	108	Horst Muhlmann

Key Additions:
Ron Carpenter (draft), Rufus Mayes (trade), Lemar Parrish (draft), Mike Reid (draft)

Starting Lineup

OFFENSE	POSITION	DEFENSE	POSITION
Virgil Carter	QB	Royce Berry	DE
Paul Robinson	RB	Mike Reid	DT
Jess Phillips	RB	Steve Chomyszak	DT
Eric Crabtree	WR	Ron Carpenter	DE
Speedy Thomas	WR	Al Beauchamp	OLB
Bob Trumpy	TE	Bill Bergey	MLB
Ernie Wright	LT	Ken Avery	OLB
Rufus Mayes	LG	Lemar Parrish	CB
Bob Johnson	C	Ken Riley	CB
Pat Matson	RG	Fletcher Smith	SS
Mike Wilson	RT	Ken Dyer	FS

SPECIAL TEAMS	POSITION
Horst Muhlmann	K
Lemar Parrish	KR
Dave Lewis	P
Lemar Parrish	PR

Lemar Parrish (left) was named to six Pro Bowls in eight seasons with the Cincinnati Bengals.

Paul Brown

Paul Brown spent 17 seasons with the Cleveland Browns, posting a 158–48–8 record and winning seven championships. More than that, he changed the NFL game as we know it. Brown was the first to hire a full-time coaching staff. He used intelligence tests when evaluating prospects, and he relied on film to evaluate and teach his players.

Nevertheless, the time for a change came in Cleveland, so owner Art Modell fired him after the 1962 season. It turned out to be wonderful news for the City of Cincinnati. Brown founded the Bengals, and his new team joined the AFL in 1968.

Brown coached the team for eight seasons, winning three division titles in the process. His Bengals won their first division title in 1970, just their third season of existence—the fastest division title by an expansion team in NFL history.

The feat was even more impressive because Brown had to re-invent his team's offense after franchise quarterback Greg Cook suffered a career-altering injury to his rotator cuff during the 1969 season. With Cook out of the mix, Brown adjusted his offense to fit quarterback Virgil Carter. (That style of offense is now called the "West Coast" offense, but it was referred to as the "Ohio River" offense at the time.)

After posting a .500 or better record in five of eight seasons with the Bengals, Brown retired from coaching in 1975 at age 67. However, his impact on football in Cincinnati was just getting started. As owner and general manager, he helped the Bengals win four division titles between 1981 and 1990, as well as two AFC championships. He remained the team's owner until he passed away in 1991 at age 82.

Brown was elected to the Pro Football Hall of Fame in 1967. He was an inaugural inductee into Cincinnati's Ring of Honor during the 2021 season. The Bengals home stadium was named Paul Brown Stadium from 2000 to 2022.

Brown talks strategy with quarterback and future Bengals coach Sam Wyche.

4–10
Fourth in AFC Central

The Bengals took a big step backward in 1971, going from first to worst in the AFC Central Division.

The season started well for Cincinnati. They crushed the Philadelphia Eagles, 37–14, in the opener at Riverfront Stadium. Quarterback Virgil Carter threw three touchdown passes, including a 90-yard strike to wide receiver Speedy Thomas. The defense forced four turnovers in the blowout victory.

The Bengals lost the next seven games, including five losses by four points or fewer. Cincinnati won three straight to improve their record to 4–7. But they dropped the final three games of the year to finish at 4–10, the team's worst record since their inaugural season in 1968.

In 10 games, Carter completed an NFL-leading 62.2% of his passes for 1,624 yards with 10 touchdowns and seven interceptions. He missed four games due to injury, which allowed head coach Paul Brown and the entire organization to get their first look at rookie quarterback Ken Anderson.

The Bengals drafted Anderson in the third round (67th overall) of the 1971 NFL Draft. His first touchdown pass came in the fourth quarter of a 20–17 loss to the Green Bay Packers, when he tossed a five-yard score to wide receiver Eric Crabtree. His best overall performance as a rookie came against the Oakland Raiders in Week 6 when he completed 14 of 20 passes for 160 yards, two touchdowns, and one interception.

Cincinnati finished 0–4 in Anderson's starts, but he played well enough to earn a chance to compete for the starting job in 1972.

Lemar Parrish was the Bengals' lone Pro Bowl player. He led the team with seven interceptions, two fumble recoveries, and two defensive touchdowns. Defensive tackle Mike Reid had a breakout season after being selected seventh overall in 1970. He finished with a team-leading 12 sacks.

Tight end Bob Trumpy led the team with 40 receptions for 531 yards and added three scores. Tight end Bruce Coslet (who would later become an offensive coordinator and head coach of the Bengals) finished second on the team with 21 catches for 356 yards and four scores.

Schedule

	OPPONENT	SCORE	RECORD
W	Philadelphia Eagles	37–14	1–0
L	@ Pittsburgh Steelers	10–21	1–1
L	@ Green Bay Packers	17–20	1–2
L	Miami Dolphins	13–23	1–3
L	Cleveland Browns	24–27	1–4
L	@ Oakland Raiders	27–31	1–5
L	@ Houston Oilers	6–10	1–6
L	Atlanta Falcons	6–9	1–7
W	@ Denver Broncos	24–10	2–7
W	Houston Oilers	28–13	3–7
W	San Diego Chargers	31–0	4–7
L	@ Cleveland Browns	27–31	4–8
L	Pittsburgh Steelers	13–21	4–9
L	@ New York Jets	21–35	4–10

Season Leaders

CATEGORY	TOTAL	PLAYER
Passing Yards	1,624	Virgil Carter
Rushing Yards	590	Fred Willis
Receiving Yards	531	Bob Trumpy
Receptions	40	Bob Trumpy
Interceptions	7	Lemar Parrish
Sacks	12	Mike Reid
Points	91	Horst Muhlmann

Key Additions:
Ken Anderson (draft), Neal Craig (draft), Vern Holland (draft)

Starting Lineup

Paul Robinson (RB)

Virgil Carter (QB)

Jess Phillips (RB)

Eric Crabtree (WR) — (CB) Ken Riley

Ernie Wright (LT) — (DE) Ron Carpenter

Howard Fest (LG) — (DT) Steve Chomyszak

Bob Johnson (C)

Pat Matson (RG) — (DT) Mike Reid

Vern Holland (RT) — (DE) Royce Berry

Bob Trumpy (TE)

Speedy Thomas (WR) — (CB) Lemar Parrish

(LB) Ken Avery

(LB) Bill Bergey

(LB) Al Beauchamp

(SS) Fletcher Smith

(FS) Sandy Durko

K   Horst Muhlmann
KR Paul Robinson
P   Dave Lewis
PR Lemar Parrish

Bengals Trivia

Ken Anderson holds no less than 18 team records, including career passing yards (32,838).

Pro Bowl Selections

• Lemar Parrish (CB)

8–6
Third in AFC Central

A head of the 1972 regular season, the quarterback battle stole the preseason spotlight. Ken Anderson went head-to-head against Virgil Carter for the starting position. Anderson won the job and went on to start 13 of 14 games. Carter's lone start came against the Chicago Bears in Week 11.

Behind the second-year quarterback, the Bengals began the season 5–2, which included blowout wins over the New England Patriots and Houston Oilers. A three-game losing streak dropped Cincinnati to 5–5. The Bengals then won back-to-back games to remain in the playoff race. They needed to beat Cleveland in Week 13 to keep their postseason hopes alive.

In that game, Anderson was injured after throwing just 10 passes. However, the Bengals led, 17–14, following a nine-yard touchdown run by Essex Johnson. Later, the Browns took a 27–24 lead on Don Cockroft's 27-yard field goal in the fourth quarter. Cincinnati drove downfield for a chance to tie or win the game, but Carter threw an interception at the goal line with just 36 seconds remaining, ending the team's playoff hopes.

The Bengals closed the season with a 61–17 win in Houston, which is tied for the most points scored in a single game in team history.

Anderson established himself as the quarterback of the present and future. Defensive tackle Mike Reid made his first Pro Bowl and was named a first-team All-Pro after finishing with 12 sacks for a second straight season. Rookie safety Tommy Casanova was named team MVP, finishing with five interceptions and a sack. Lemar Parrish also had five interceptions and returned two for touchdowns.

The Bengals finished 13th in the NFL in points scored (299) and fifth in points allowed (229).

Pro Bowl Selections

- Chip Myers (WR)
- Mike Reid (DT)

Schedule

OPPONENT	SCORE	RECORD
W @ New England Patriots	31–7	1–0
W Pittsburgh Steelers	15–10	2–0
L @ Cleveland Browns	6–27	2–1
W Denver Broncos	21–10	3–1
W @ Kansas City Chiefs	23–16	4–1
L @ Los Angeles Rams	12–15	4–2
W Houston Oilers	30–7	5–2
L @ Pittsburgh Steelers	17–40	5–3
L Oakland Raiders	14–20	5–4
L Baltimore Colts	19–20	5–5
W @ Chicago Bears	13–3	6–5
W New York Giants	13–10	7–5
L Cleveland Browns	24–27	7–6
W @ Houston Oilers	61–17	8–6

Season Leaders

CATEGORY	TOTAL	PLAYER
Passing Yards	1,918	Ken Anderson
Rushing Yards	825	Essex Johnson
Receiving Yards	792	Chip Myers
Receptions	57	Chip Myers
Interceptions	5	T. Casanova, L. Parrish
Sacks	12	Mike Reid
Points	111	Horst Muhlmann

Key Additions:
Tommy Casanova (draft), Charlie Joiner (trade), Jim LeClair (draft), Sherman White (draft)

Mike Reid posted an impressive 49 sacks in just 63 career games.

Starting Lineup

OFFENSE	POSITION
Ken Anderson	QB
Essex Johnson	RB
Doug Dressler	RB
Chip Myers	WR
Speedy Thomas	WR
Bob Trumpy	TE
Stan Walters	LT
Howard Fest	LG
Bob Johnson	C
Pat Matson	RG
Vern Holland	RT

DEFENSE	POSITION
Royce Berry	DE
Mike Reid	DT
Steve Chomyszak	DT
Sherman White	DE
Al Beauchamp	OLB
Bill Bergey	MLB
Ken Avery	OLB
Lemar Parrish	CB
Ken Riley	CB
Neal Craig	SS
Tommy Casanova	FS

SPECIAL TEAMS	POSITION
Horst Muhlmann	K
Bernard Jackson	KR
Dave Lewis	P
Tommy Casanova	PR

10–4
First in AFC Central

Cincinnati started the 1973 season in average fashion, going 4–4. That included back-to-back losses to the Pittsburgh Steelers and Dallas Cowboys in Weeks 7 and 8.

Kicker Horst Muhlmann's 33-yard field goal propelled the Bengals past the Buffalo Bills, 16–13, in Week 9. Then the Bengals took off, winning six straight games. They closed out the season with a 27–24 road win over the Houston Oilers to secure the AFC Central Division championship.

Cincinnati's rivalry with Pittsburgh was officially born in 1973. The teams split their two regular-season matchups, and Steelers star quarterback Terry Bradshaw said, "I'd really rather beat Cincinnati than anybody." The Steelers finished with an identical 10–4 record, but the Bengals won the division due to a tiebreaker. (They had a better record against AFC opponents.)

The Bengals played the 12–2 Dolphins in Miami in the Divisional Round of the playoffs. Cincinnati lost star running back Essex Johnson on the first series, and the Dolphins took command early, building a 21–3 lead in the second quarter. A 45-yard interception return for a touchdown by safety Neal Craig gave the Bengals some momentum. Cincinnati scored 13 straight points but still trailed at halftime, 21–16. Unfortunately for the Bengals, their offense couldn't get anything going in the second half. Miami outscored Cincinnati 13–0 to secure a 34–16 win.

That game had a lasting impact on the NFL. The Dolphins were able to shut down sensational rookie receiver Isaac Curtis by continually hitting him well past the line of scrimmage. So, that offseason, Paul Brown pushed for the Isaac Curtis Rule. It was approved, and defenders could no longer impede wide receivers more than five yards beyond the line of scrimmage.

Boobie Clark, a 12th-round draft pick, was named AFC Rookie of the Year.

Pro Bowl Selections

- Isaac Curtis (WR)
- Mike Reid (DT)
- Bob Trumpy (TE)

Schedule

	OPPONENT	SCORE	RECORD
L	@ Denver Broncos	10–28	0–1
W	Houston Oilers	24–10	1–1
W	@ San Diego Chargers	20–13	2–1
L	@ Cleveland Browns	10–17	2–2
W	Pittsburgh Steelers	19–7	3–2
W	Kansas City Chiefs	14–6	4–2
L	@ Pittsburgh Steelers	13–20	4–3
L	@ Dallas Cowboys	10–38	4–4
W	@ Buffalo Bills	16–13	5–4
W	New York Jets	20–14	6–4
W	Saint Louis Cardinals	42–24	7–4
W	Minnesota Vikings	27–0	8–4
W	Cleveland Browns	34–17	9–4
W	@ Houston Oilers	27–24	10–4
L	*@ Miami Dolphins*	*16–34*	*0–1*

Season Leaders

CATEGORY	TOTAL	PLAYER
Passing Yards	2,428	Ken Anderson
Rushing Yards	997	Essex Johnson
Receiving Yards	843	Isaac Curtis
Receptions	45	B. Clark, I. Curtis
Interceptions	4	Tommy Casanova
Sacks	13	Mike Reid
Points	94	Horst Muhlmann

Key Additions:
Boobie Clark (draft), Isaac Curtis (draft)

Starting Lineup

OFFENSE	POSITION
Ken Anderson	QB
Essex Johnson	RB
Boobie Clark	RB
Isaac Curtis	WR
Tim George	WR
Bob Trumpy	TE
Rufus Mayes	LT
Howard Fest	LG
Bob Johnson	C
Pat Matson	RG
Vern Holland	RT

DEFENSE	POSITION
Royce Berry	DE
Mike Reid	DT
Ron Carpenter	DT
Sherman White	DE
Al Beauchamp	OLB
Bill Bergey	MLB
Ron Pritchard	OLB
Lemar Parrish	CB
Ken Riley	CB
Neal Craig	SS
Tommy Casanova	FS

SPECIAL TEAMS	POSITION
Horst Muhlmann	K
Bernard Jackson	KR
Dave Lewis	P
Lemar Parrish	PR

Bill Bergey (66) was named to six Pro Bowls in his 12-year NFL career.

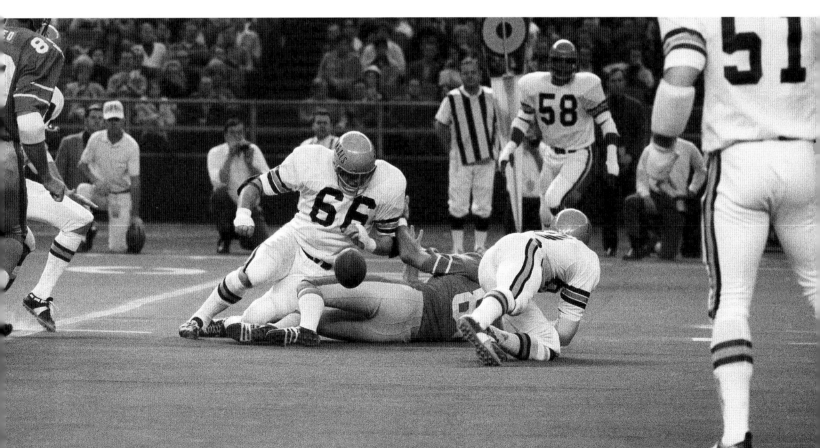

7–7
Third in AFC Central

The Bengals had one of the NFL's most exciting offenses in 1974, and Ken Anderson emerged as one of the best quarterbacks. The 25-year-old led the league in completions (213), completion percentage (64.9), and passing yards (2,667).

Anderson and the Bengals started the season strong, scoring 28 or more points in three of their first five contests. They began the year 4–1, which included two wins over the Cleveland Browns. The Bengals swept the "Battle of Ohio" for the first time in franchise history.

Cincinnati split the next four contests, with losses to the Oakland Raiders and Houston Oilers, but they remained on track to make another playoff run after winning the division the previous year.

In Week 9 versus the Pittsburgh Steelers, Anderson completed a Bengals' record 90.9% of his passes (20 of 22). He threw for 227 yards and led his team to a 17–10 victory.

Cincinnati's most dominant performance came against the Kansas City Chiefs in Week 11. The offense rolled with 438 yards, including 268 yards passing and four touchdowns from Anderson. Meanwhile, the defense stifled Len Dawson and the Chiefs, holding them to 174 yards in a 33–6 win.

Standing at 7–4, the Bengals were poised for a postseason push. Instead, they suffered a late-season collapse. They dropped their final three games, including blowout losses to the Miami Dolphins and the Steelers. It was a disappointing end to what had been an exciting season in Cincinnati.

Exemplifying their .500 record on the season, the Bengals were middle-of-the-road in total offense and total defense. They finished 10th in points scored (283) and 13th in points against (259).

Wide receiver Isaac Curtis made the Pro Bowl for a second straight year, finishing with 30 catches for 633 yards and 10 touchdowns. Cornerback Lemar Parrish made his third Pro Bowl. He led the NFL in punt returns, averaging an incredible 18.8 yards per return—still a franchise record. He returned two punts for touchdowns on the season, including one that went for 90 yards.

Schedule

	OPPONENT	SCORE	RECORD
W	Cleveland Browns	33–7	1–0
L	San Diego Chargers	17–20	1–1
W	@ San Francisco 49ers	21–3	2–1
W	Washington	28–17	3–1
W	@ Cleveland Browns	34–24	4–1
L	@ Oakland Raiders	27–30	4–2
L	Houston Oilers	21–34	4–3
W	@ Baltimore Colts	24–14	5–3
W	Pittsburgh Steelers	17–10	6–3
L	@ Houston Oilers	3–20	6–4
W	Kansas City Chiefs	33–6	7–4
L	@ Miami Dolphins	3–24	7–5
L	Detroit Lions	19–23	7–6
L	@ Pittsburgh Steelers	3–27	7–7

Season Leaders

CATEGORY	TOTAL	PLAYER
Passing Yards	2,667	Ken Anderson
Rushing Yards	375	Charlie Davis
Receiving Yards	633	Isaac Curtis
Receptions	32	Chip Myers
Interceptions	5	Ken Riley
Sacks	13	Ron Carpenter
Points	65	Horst Muhlmann

Key Additions:
Dave Lapham (draft)

Starting Lineup

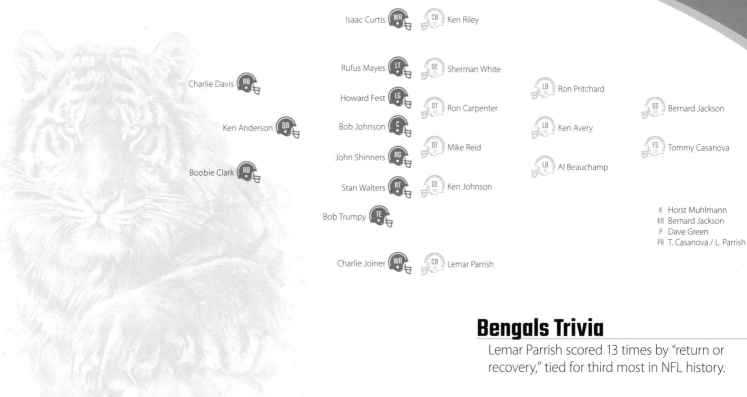

Isaac Curtis (WR) — (CB) Ken Riley

Charlie Davis (RB)

Rufus Mayes (LT) — (DE) Sherman White

Howard Fest (LG)

Ken Anderson (QB) — (DT) Ron Carpenter

Bob Johnson (C)

Boobie Clark (RB)

John Shinners (RG) — (DT) Mike Reid

Stan Walters (RT) — (DE) Ken Johnson

Bob Trumpy (TE)

Charlie Joiner (WR) — (CB) Lemar Parrish

(LB) Ron Pritchard

(LB) Ken Avery

(LB) Al Beauchamp

(SS) Bernard Jackson

(FS) Tommy Casanova

K   Horst Muhlmann
KR Bernard Jackson
P   Dave Green
PR T. Casanova / L. Parrish

Bengals Trivia

Lemar Parrish scored 13 times by "return or recovery," tied for third most in NFL history.

Pro Bowl Selections

- Tommy Casanova (S)
- Isaac Curtis (WR)
- Lemar Parrish (CB)

Parrish Sets Punt-Return Record

1974

11–3
Second in AFC Central

The 1975 campaign was Paul Brown's final season as head coach of the Bengals. The team finished with their best record up to that point, 11–3, and they qualified for the playoffs for the third time in franchise history.

Quarterback Ken Anderson had his best year yet, leading the NFL with 3,169 yards. Cincinnati finished in the top 10 in scoring offense (9th) and defense (6th) for just the second time in franchise history (1970).

The Bengals started the season 6–0, which included blowout wins over the New Orleans Saints and New England Patriots. Despite their success, they still struggled against the rival Pittsburgh Steelers. They lost to Pittsburgh, 30–24, in Week 7 at home and then lost again, 35–14, in Week 13.

The Bengals split with the Cleveland Browns and swept the Houston Oilers to finish 3–3 in AFC Central play. They cruised past the San Diego Chargers in Week 14 to set up a playoff showdown against John Madden's Raiders.

The game was played in the Oakland Coliseum. The home team got off to a quick start and held off a late rally by the Bengals to win, 31–28. It was Cincinnati's first and only loss outside of the division in 1975.

Pro Bowl defensive tackle Mike Reid retired before the start of the season to pursue a career in music. He would go on to win a Grammy Award for Best Country Song with "Stranger in My House." He released three studio albums and worked with Alabama, Marie Osmond, Collin Raye, and Conway Twitty.

Anderson became the first Bengals player to win the NFL Man of the Year Award, which honors players for their volunteer and charity work. Isaac Curtis was named to his third straight Pro Bowl and finished with a career-high 934 receiving yards.

Pro Bowl Selections

- Ken Anderson (QB)
- Isaac Curtis (WR)
- Lemar Parrish (CB)

Schedule

	OPPONENT	SCORE	RECORD
W	Cleveland Browns	24–17	1–0
W	@ New Orleans Saints	21–0	2–0
W	@ Houston Oilers	21–19	3–0
W	New England Patriots	27–10	4–0
W	Oakland Raiders	14–10	5–0
W	@ Atlanta Falcons	21–14	6–0
L	Pittsburgh Steelers	24–30	6–1
W	@ Denver Broncos	17–16	7–1
W	Buffalo Bills	33–24	8–1
L	@ Cleveland Browns	23–35	8–2
W	Houston Oilers	23–19	9–2
W	@ Philadelphia Eagles	31–0	10–2
L	@ Pittsburgh Steelers	14–35	10–3
W	San Diego Chargers	47–17	11–3
L	*@ Oakland Raiders*	*28–31*	*0–1*

Season Leaders

CATEGORY	TOTAL	PLAYER
Passing Yards	3,169	Ken Anderson
Rushing Yards	594	Boobie Clark
Receiving Yards	934	Isaac Curtis
Receptions	44	Isaac Curtis
Interceptions	6	Ken Riley
Sacks	7.5	Sherman White
Points	70	Dave Green

Key Additions:
Glenn Cameron (draft), Marvin Cobb (draft), Bo Harris (draft), Pat McInally (draft)

Isaac Curtis led the NFL with an average of 21.2 yards per reception.

Starting Lineup

OFFENSE	POSITION
Ken Anderson	QB
Stan Fritts	RB
Boobie Clark	RB
Isaac Curtis	WR
Charlie Joiner	WR
Bob Trumpy	TE
Rufus Mayes	LT
Howard Fest	LG
Bob Johnson	C
Dave Lapham	RG
Vern Holland	RT

DEFENSE	POSITION
Ken Johnson	DE
Robert Brown	DT
Ron Carpenter	DT
Sherman White	DE
Al Beauchamp	OLB
Jim LeClair	MLB
Ron Pritchard	OLB
Lemar Parrish	CB
Ken Riley	CB
Tommy Casanova	SS
Bernard Jackson	FS

SPECIAL TEAMS	POSITION
Dave Green	K
Bernard Jackson	KR
Dave Green	P
Lyle Blackwood	PR

10–4
Second in AFC Central

Paul Brown officially retired from coaching on January 1, 1976. He posted a 55–56–1 record in eight seasons in Cincinnati and a 213–104–9 overall mark during his 25 seasons of coaching professional football. Offensive line coach Bill "Tiger" Johnson was named Brown's successor as the Bengals' head coach.

His team started fast, winning four of their first five games. After dropping a Week 6 contest in Pittsburgh, Cincinnati rattled off five consecutive wins to get to 9–2 on the year.

The Steelers had snapped the Bengals' three-game winning streak earlier in the season, and they did the same thing in Week 12. Cincinnati lost, 7–3, to their division rival at Riverfront Stadium. The Bengals scored just nine points in two games against the Steelers, and it ultimately cost them a spot in the postseason. They lost the playoff tiebreaker to the 10–4 Steelers. Cincinnati's .714 winning percentage remains the highest of any team in Bengals history that didn't qualify for the playoffs.

Before the season, Cincinnati traded future hall-of-famer Charlie Joiner to the San Diego Chargers in exchange for Coy Bacon. The defensive end finished 1976 with 21.5 sacks, the most in franchise history. He only spent two seasons in Cincinnati but made the Pro Bowl both years.

Cornerback Ken Riley led the AFC with nine interceptions, including a 53-yard pick-six in Week 3 against the Packers. He had a career-high three interceptions in Week 14 against the Jets.

The Bengals offense was one of the best in the NFL, averaging 23.9 points per game, sixth in the league. The defense held opponents to just 15 points per game, which ranked seventh in the NFL.

Pro Bowl Selections

- Ken Anderson (QB)
- Coy Bacon (DE)
- Tommy Casanova (S)
- Isaac Curtis (WR)
- Jim LeClair (LB)
- Lemar Parrish (CB)

Schedule

OPPONENT	SCORE	RECORD
W Denver Broncos	17–7	1–0
L @ Baltimore Colts	27–28	1–1
W Green Bay Packers	28–7	2–1
W @ Cleveland Browns	45–24	3–1
W Tampa Bay Buccaneers	21–0	4–1
L @ Pittsburgh Steelers	6–23	4–2
W @ Houston Oilers	27–7	5–2
W Cleveland Browns	21–6	6–2
W Los Angeles Rams	20–12	7–2
W Houston Oilers	31–27	8–2
W @ Kansas City Chiefs	27–24	9–2
L Pittsburgh Steelers	3–7	9–3
L @ Oakland Raiders	20–35	9–4
W @ New York Jets	42–3	10–4

Season Leaders

CATEGORY	TOTAL	PLAYER
Passing Yards	2,367	Ken Anderson
Rushing Yards	671	Boobie Clark
Receiving Yards	766	Isaac Curtis
Receptions	41	Isaac Curtis
Interceptions	9	Ken Riley
Sacks	21.5	Coy Bacon
Points	81	Chris Bahr

Key Additions:
Coy Bacon (trade), Glenn Bujnoch (draft), Archie Griffin (draft), Reggie Williams (draft)

Starting Lineup

OFFENSE	POSITION
Ken Anderson	QB
Archie Griffin	RB
Boobie Clark	RB
Isaac Curtis	WR
Billy Brooks	WR
Bob Trumpy	TE
Rufus Mayes	LT
John Shinners	LG
Bob Johnson	C
Dave Lapham	RG
Vern Holland	RT

DEFENSE	POSITION
Gary Burley	DE
Robert Brown	DT
Ron Carpenter	DT
Coy Bacon	DE
Bo Harris	OLB
Jim LeClair	MLB
Reggie Williams	OLB
Lemar Parrish	CB
Ken Riley	CB
Tommy Casanova	SS
Marvin Cobb	FS

SPECIAL TEAMS	POSITION
Chris Bahr	K
Willie Shelby	KR
Pat McInally	P
Willie Shelby	PR

"When you win,
say nothing.
When you lose,
say less."

—Paul Brown

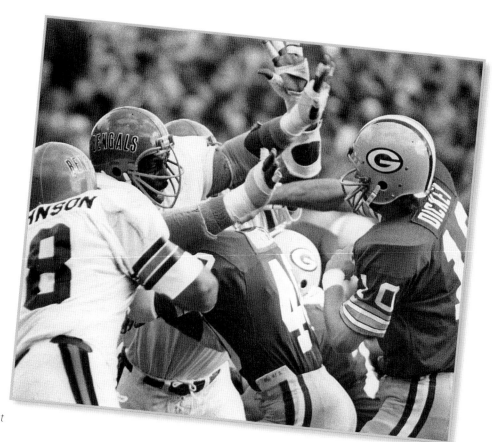

Coy Bacon had 27 sacks in just 26 games with the Bengals.

Ken Anderson

Ken Anderson remains one of the greatest players in franchise history. The legendary quarterback led Cincinnati to Super Bowl XVI in 1981, becoming the first Bengals player to win the NFL MVP Award in the process. He saw action in 192 regular-season games with Cincinnati, and he was named to four Pro Bowls.

Anderson led the NFL in completion percentage three times (1974, 1982, 1983). He led the league in passing yards twice (1974, 1975) and in completions twice (1974, 1982). He also led the NFL in quarterback rating four times (1974, 1975, 1981, 1982). Anderson is one of only five players in league history to win four passing titles. He's the only player to win back-to-back passing titles in two different decades.

Anderson is still the longest-tenured Bengals player in team history, spending 16 seasons with Cincinnati. He saw limited action during his rookie season, and he only started two games in the last two years of his career, but from 1972 to 1984, he was the Bengals' starting quarterback. He threw for 32,838 yards, which is still the most in team history.

Anderson was known for his accuracy, competitiveness, and ability to make any throw on the field. He and wide receiver Isaac Curtis formed one of the NFL's best duos of the 1970s. He had that same rapport with receiver Cris Collinsworth in the early 1980s.

Anderson was an inaugural inductee in the Bengals Ring of Honor in 2021, joining Paul Brown, Anthony Munoz, and Ken Riley. Anderson's precision, leadership, longevity, and on-field success are all reasons why he's considered one of the best ever to don the orange and black.

8–6
Second in AFC Central

The Bengals finished with a winning record for a third straight season in 1977, but it wasn't enough to qualify for the playoffs. Cincinnati posted an 8–6 record, finishing second in the AFC Central behind the Pittsburgh Steelers.

The Bengals got off to a rocky start, dropping four of their first six games. But an overtime win over the Houston Oilers completely changed their season. Chris Bahr's 22-yard field goal gave Cincinnati the victory—and new momentum.

The Bengals beat the Cleveland Browns the following week to get back to .500 and then won four straight games late in the year to get to 8–5.

Cincinnati's 17–10 victory over Pittsburgh in Week 13 snapped a six-game losing streak to the Steelers. The Bengals held their division rival scoreless in the second half to secure the win.

They just needed to beat Houston again to clinch the AFC Central Division championship. But the Oilers won, 21–16, despite being 3.5-point underdogs going into the game.

Ken Anderson led the team in passing with 2,145 yards, 11 touchdowns, and 11 interceptions. His 51.4% completion percentage was a career low.

Cincinnati's backfield tandem of Pete Johnson and Archie Griffin combined for 1,134 rushing yards. Johnson also had four rushing touchdowns, and Griffin hauled in 28 catches for 240 yards.

Legendary tight end Bob Trumpy retired after the 1977 season. Star safety Tommy Casanova surprisingly retired before training camp began in 1978, in order to become an eye surgeon. He was only 27 years old and was coming off back-to-back Pro Bowl seasons.

Pro Bowl Selections

- Coy Bacon (DE)
- Tommy Casanova (S)
- Lemar Parrish (CB)

Schedule

OPPONENT	SCORE	RECORD
L Cleveland Browns	3–13	0–1
W Seattle Seahawks	42–20	1–1
L @ San Diego Chargers	3–24	1–2
W @ Green Bay Packers	17–7	2–2
L @ Pittsburgh Steelers	14–20	2–3
L Denver Broncos	13–24	2–4
W Houston Oilers (OT)	13–10	3–4
W @ Cleveland Browns	10–7	4–4
L @ Minnesota Vikings	10–42	4–5
W Miami Dolphins	23–17	5–5
W New York Giants	30–13	6–5
W @ Kansas City Chiefs	27–7	7–5
W Pittsburgh Steelers	17–10	8–5
L @ Houston Oilers	16–21	8–6

Season Leaders

CATEGORY	TOTAL	PLAYER
Passing Yards	2,145	Ken Anderson
Rushing Yards	585	Pete Johnson
Receiving Yards	772	Billy Brooks
Receptions	39	Billy Brooks
Interceptions	3	L. Parrish, R. Williams
Sacks	9.5	Gary Burley
Points	82	Chris Bahr

Key Additions:
Louis Breeden (draft), Eddie Edwards (draft), Pete Johnson (draft), Wilson Whitley (draft)

Starting Lineup

OFFENSE	POSITION
Ken Anderson	QB
Archie Griffin	RB
Pete Johnson	RB
Isaac Curtis	WR
Billy Brooks	WR
Bob Trumpy	TE
Rufus Mayes	LT
Glenn Bujnoch	LG
Bob Johnson	C
Dave Lapham	RG
Vern Holland	RT

DEFENSE	POSITION
Gary Burley	DE
Eddie Edwards	DT
Wilson Whitley	DT
Coy Bacon	DE
Bo Harris	OLB
Jim LeClair	MLB
Reggie Williams	OLB
Lemar Parrish	CB
Ken Riley	CB
Tommy Casanova	SS
Marvin Cobb	FS

SPECIAL TEAMS	POSITION
Chris Bahr	K
Willie Shelby	KR
Pat McInally	P
Tony Davis	PR

Tommy Casanova was a sure tackler. He was named to three Pro Bowls in his career.

4–12
Fourth in AFC Central

The NFL went to 16-game seasons in 1978. Unfortunately for the Bengals, those extra games didn't result in more wins. They got off to a bad start and never recovered.

Star quarterback Ken Anderson missed the first four games with a broken right hand, and the team started 0–8. The Bengals were competitive, though. Five of those losses were one-possession games.

Head coach Bill "Tiger" Johnson resigned after the Week 5 loss to the San Francisco 49ers. Quarterbacks coach Homer Rice was named Cincinnati's interim head coach.

After falling to Buffalo by the unusual score of 5–0, the Bengals beat the Oilers, 28–13, in Week 9 to pick up their first win. Cincinnati couldn't build any momentum following the victory. They lost four more contests before finishing the season with three straight wins. The team ended on a high note, blowing out the Cleveland Browns, 48–16. That game showcased the talents of Cincinnati's dynamic duo of running backs. Pete Johnson set a franchise record, rushing for 160 yards. Meanwhile, Archie Griffin added 65 yards rushing, caught a touchdown pass, and threw a touchdown pass too.

It was Anderson's worst season as a starter. He threw for 2,219 yards, 10 touchdowns, and 22 interceptions in 12 games. A 58.0 quarterback rating was his lowest during his 13 seasons as the Bengals' starting quarterback.

Johnson ran for a team-high 762 yards and seven touchdowns. Isaac Curtis led the way at receiver, finishing with 47 receptions for 737 yards.

The Bengals struggled to score, averaging 15.8 points per game (21st in the NFL). They finished with just four wins for the third time in team history and for the first time since 1971.

Paul Brown opted to keep Rice on as head coach after he led Cincinnati to three wins at the end of the season.

Pro Bowl Selections

• None

Schedule

OPPONENT	SCORE	RECORD
L Kansas City Chiefs	23–24	0–1
L @ Cleveland Browns (OT)	10–13	0–2
L Pittsburgh Steelers	3–28	0–3
L New Orleans Saints	18–20	0–4
L @ San Francisco 49ers	12–28	0–5
L @ Miami Dolphins	0–21	0–6
L New England Patriots	3–10	0–7
L @ Buffalo Bills	0–5	0–8
W Houston Oilers	28–13	1–8
L @ San Diego Chargers	13–22	1–9
L Oakland Raiders	21–34	1–10
L @ Pittsburgh Steelers	6–7	1–11
L @ Houston Oilers	10–17	1–12
W Atlanta Falcons	37–7	2–12
W @ Los Angeles Rams	20–19	3–12
W Cleveland Browns	48–16	4–12

Season Leaders

CATEGORY	TOTAL	PLAYER
Passing Yards	2,219	Ken Anderson
Rushing Yards	762	Pete Johnson
Receiving Yards	737	Isaac Curtis
Receptions	47	Isaac Curtis
Interceptions	4	Dick Jauron
Sacks	8	Ross Browner
Points	74	Chris Bahr

Key Additions:
Ross Browner (draft), Blair Bush (draft)

Starting Lineup

OFFENSE	POSITION
Ken Anderson	QB
Archie Griffin	RB
Pete Johnson	RB
Isaac Curtis	WR
Billy Brooks	WR
Don Bass	TE
Mike Wilson	LT
Glenn Bujnoch	LG
Blair Bush	C
Dave Lapham	RG
Vern Holland	RT

DEFENSE	POSITION
Gary Burley	DE
Wilson Whitley	DT
Eddie Edwards	DT
Ross Browner	DE
Glenn Cameron	OLB
Jim LeClair	MLB
Reggie Williams	OLB
Louis Breeden	CB
Ken Riley	CB
Marvin Cobb	SS
Scott Perry	FS

SPECIAL TEAMS	POSITION
Chris Bahr	K
Ray Griffin	KR
Pat McInally	P
Dennis Law/Tony Davis	PR

Jim LeClair spent his entire 12-year career with the Bengals and started 128 games.

4–12
Fourth in AFC Central

The Bengals stuck with Homer Rice as head coach, removing the "interim" tag and making it official. The continuity did not lead to wins. Cincinnati once again posted a 4–12 record and finished last in the AFC Central.

The team started the year 0–6 with blowout losses to the Buffalo Bills and Dallas Cowboys. The Bengals' first win came in Week 7 against Pittsburgh at Riverfront Stadium. It was perhaps the most shocking blowout upset in NFL history. The Steelers were at the height of their dynasty and had won 23 of their last 25 games, including the previous Super Bowl. Meanwhile, Cincinnati entered the game at 0–6, with the NFL's worst point differential (-74). Yet after falling behind, 3–0, the Bengals went on to score 34 straight points (aided by nine Pittsburgh turnovers) and ultimately won, 34–10.

The Bengals crushed the Philadelphia Eagles two weeks later to improve to 2–7, but they failed to win back-to-back games in a season for the first time in franchise history.

Center Blair Bush suffered a knee injury late in the year, so Paul Brown convinced former great Bob Johnson to come out of retirement. Johnson, 33, had been the first draft pick in team history. He served as the long snapper on punts, extra points, and field goals for the final five games. Johnson started 136 games in 12 years with the Bengals. His number 54 remains the only number retired by the franchise.

Running back Pete Johnson was a bright spot in 1979, running for a career-high 14 touchdowns. Ken Anderson bounced back a year after throwing 22 interceptions. He finished with 16 touchdowns and 10 picks.

The Bengals selected quarterback Jack Thompson with the third overall pick in the 1979 NFL Draft. Nicknamed the "Throwin' Samoan," Thompson started one game and made nine appearances as a rookie.

The Bengals parted ways with Rice following the 1979 campaign. He posted an 8–19 record in two seasons as head coach. They named Forrest Gregg the fourth head coach in team history on December 28, 1979. The Bengals nabbed the 46-year-old from the Toronto Argonauts of the Canadian Football League. It was a move that would quickly pay off for Cincinnati.

Schedule

	OPPONENT	SCORE	RECORD
L	@ Denver Broncos	0–10	0–1
L	@ Buffalo Bills	24–51	0–2
L	New England Patriots	14–20	0–3
L	Houston Oilers (OT)	27–30	0–4
L	@ Dallas Cowboys	13–38	0–5
L	Kansas City Chiefs	7–10	0–6
W	Pittsburgh Steelers	34–10	1–6
L	@ Cleveland Browns	27–28	1–7
W	Philadelphia Eagles	37–13	2–7
L	@ Baltimore Colts	28–38	2–8
L	San Diego Chargers	24–26	2–9
L	@ Houston Oilers	21–42	2–10
W	Saint Louis Cardinals	34–28	3–10
L	@ Pittsburgh Steelers	17–37	3–11
L	@ Washington	14–28	3–12
W	Cleveland Browns	16–12	4–12

Season Leaders

CATEGORY	TOTAL	PLAYER
Passing Yards	2,340	Ken Anderson
Rushing Yards	865	Pete Johnson
Receiving Yards	724	Don Bass
Receptions	58	Don Bass
Interceptions	6	Dick Jauron
Sacks	6	Ross Browner
Points	90	Pete Johnson

Key Additions:
Max Montoya (draft), Dan Ross (draft)

Starting Lineup

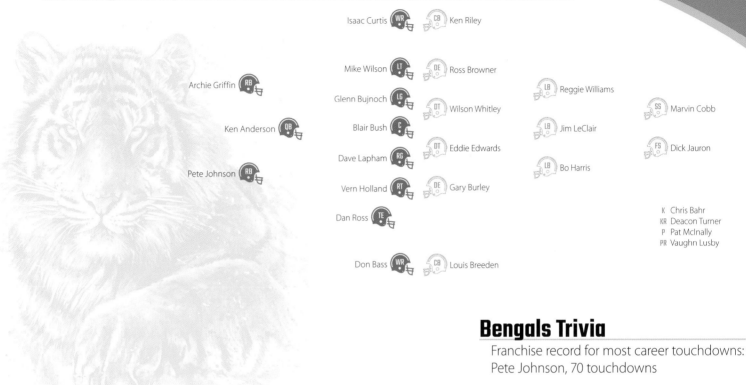

Archie Griffin RB

Ken Anderson QB

Pete Johnson RB

Isaac Curtis WR — CB Ken Riley

Mike Wilson LT — DE Ross Browner

Glenn Bujnoch LG

Blair Bush C — DT Wilson Whitley

Dave Lapham RG — DT Eddie Edwards

Vern Holland RT — DE Gary Burley

Dan Ross TE

Don Bass WR — CB Louis Breeden

LB Reggie Williams

LB Jim LeClair

LB Bo Harris

SS Marvin Cobb

FS Dick Jauron

K   Chris Bahr
KR Deacon Turner
P   Pat McInally
PR Vaughn Lusby

Bengals Trivia

Franchise record for most career touchdowns:
Pete Johnson, 70 touchdowns

Upset Blowout of Pittsburgh Steelers
1979

Pro Bowl Selections

• None

All-1970s Offense

QUARTERBACK: Ken Anderson (1971–1979) threw for 20,030 yards and 125 touchdowns. He posted a 59–52 record in 111 starts and brought stability to the quarterback position after Greg Cook suffered a career-altering shoulder injury in 1969. Anderson is the Bengals' all-time leader in passing yards (32,838) and wins (91). He ranks second in touchdowns (197).

RUNNING BACKS: Essex Johnson (1970–1975) and **Boobie Clark** (1973–1978) led the way at running back. Johnson appeared in 72 games, running for 2,838 yards and 15 touchdowns. He also had 119 receptions for 1,505 yards and 11 scores. Clark made 54 starts. He ran for 2,978 yards and 25 touchdowns. He also had 151 catches for 1,139 yards and two scores.

WIDE RECEIVERS: Anderson's favorite target was legendary wide receiver **Isaac Curtis** (1973–1979). The speedster made the Pro Bowl in each of his first four seasons. He led the NFL with 21.2 yards per catch in 1975. Curtis had 259 receptions for 4,856 yards and 45 touchdowns. **Chip Myers** (1970–1976) hauled in 208 receptions for 2,874 yards and 10 touchdowns in 82 career games in Cincinnati. Myers made the Pro Bowl in 1972 after catching 57 passes for 792 yards.

TIGHT END: Bob Trumpy (1970–1977) is considered the best tight end in team history. His 4,600 career receiving yards are the most by a Bengals tight end. He ranks third in franchise history among tight ends in receptions (298) and third in games played (128). Trumpy was a four-time Pro Bowl player and was a first-team All-Pro in 1969.

CENTER: The Bengals took center **Bob Johnson** (1970–1979) with the second overall pick in the 1968 NFL Draft, their first selection in team history. Paul Brown certainly got it right with Johnson, who went on to start 108 games at center for the Bengals in the 1970s. He was a Pro Bowl player in 1968 and remains the only player in franchise history with his number retired.

GUARDS: After spending some time at offensive tackle, **Howard Fest** (1970–1975) made his biggest impact at left guard from 1971 to 1975. He started 65 games in the 1970s. **Dave Lapham** (1974–1979) held down the right guard spot for the majority of the decade. He appeared in all 14 games as a rookie and started 69 games during the 1970s. Lapham spent 10 seasons with the Bengals and has worked as a radio analyst for the team since 1986.

TACKLES: Rufus Mayes (1970–1978) and **Vern Holland** (1971–1979) get the nod at left and right tackle, respectively. Mayes made 98 starts for the Bengals, primarily at left tackle. Holland was the Bengals' first-round pick (15th overall) in 1971. He started 118 games at right tackle over the next nine seasons.

KICKER: Horst Muhlmann (1970–1974) is the kicker of the decade after booting for the Bengals in 70 games. He made 64% of his field goal attempts and 97% of his extra points.

KICK RETURNER: Bernard Jackson (1972–1976) earned the decade's spot at kick returner after averaging 23.9 yards per return on 96 attempts, with a long of 62 yards.

Statistics for the all-decade team are for the given decade only, unless otherwise noted.

All-1970s Defense

DEFENSIVE ENDS: Royce Berry (1970–1974) and **Coy Bacon** (1976–1977) make the team at defensive end. Berry started 56 games and finished with 19 sacks. Bacon had 27 sacks in 26 starts. That included 21.5 sacks in 1976, the most in a single season in franchise history.

DEFENSIVE TACKLES: The Bengals took **Mike Reid** (1970–1974) with the seventh pick in the 1970 NFL Draft. He finished third in voting for Defensive Rookie of the Year. He had at least 12 sacks in three straight seasons from 1971 to 1973. Reid was a first-team All-Pro in 1972. **Ron Carpenter** (1970–1976) was a second-round pick in 1970. He had 45.5 career sacks, but his best two seasons were in 1973 and 1974 when he finished with 10 and 13 sacks, respectively.

LINEBACKERS: **Al Beauchamp** (1970–1975) started 83 games for the Bengals. He had 12 interceptions and also scored two defensive touchdowns. He started every game but one between 1970 and 1975. **Jim LeClair** (1972–1979) made one Pro Bowl and appeared in 106 games. The middle linebacker had eight interceptions, eight fumble recoveries, and three sacks over that span. **Ken Avery** (1970–1974) appeared in 68 games for the Bengals. He had two interceptions, three fumble recoveries, and five sacks.

CORNERBACKS: **Ken Riley** (1970–1979) is one of the best players in franchise history. He had 40 interceptions in the 1970s and was a second-team All-Pro twice. **Lemar Parrish** (1970–1977) manned the other cornerback spot and completes what might be the Bengals' all-time best DB-duo. He made six Pro Bowls in the 1970s and had 25 interceptions—four of them returned for touchdowns.

SAFETIES: Tommy Casanova (1972–1977) only spent six seasons in the NFL, but he was one of the most productive safeties in team history. Casanova had 17 career interceptions, made three Pro Bowls, and was a first-team All-Pro in 1976. **Marvin Cobb** (1975–1979) takes the other safety spot after appearing in 71 games with 54 starts. He had 13 career interceptions, one of which he returned for a touchdown.

PUNTER: Dave Lewis (1970–1973) narrowly edges out Pat McInally for the punter spot. Lewis appeared in 56 games. He was named first-team All-Pro in 1970 after leading the league in average yards per punt (46.2). He led the NFL in yards per punt again in 1971 (44.8).

PUNT RETURNER: Lemar Parrish (1970–1977) averaged 9.2 yards on 130 returns. He had four punt returns for touchdowns, which remains a franchise record, and he led the NFL with an 18.8-yard average per return in 1974.

In 10 seasons, Bob Trumpy caught 298 passes for 4,600 yards.

6–10
Fourth in AFC Central

The Bengals struggled in Forrest Gregg's first season as head coach, but a decision he made in the draft would pay off for years to come. Gregg stood on the table for University of Southern California (USC) left tackle Anthony Munoz, and the Bengals selected him with the third pick in the 1980 NFL Draft.

Injury concerns scared some teams away from Munoz. He underwent knee surgery three times in college, including once during his final collegiate season. However, Gregg was all in on Munoz.

On the field, the 1980 season was a struggle for the Bengals. They started 1–4 but rallied to a 3–4 mark. Unfortunately, the team followed that with five straight losses by double digits.

The Bengals finished 6–10, and the offense became a big question mark. Cincinnati's offense averaged 15.3 points per game, which ranked 27th out of 28 NFL teams.

Gregg went back and forth between quarterbacks Ken Anderson and Jack Thompson. Anderson threw twice as many interceptions (13) as touchdowns (6). Meanwhile, Thompson completed less than 50% of his passes and threw 12 interceptions in his second NFL season.

Cincinnati's Week 9 loss to the San Diego Chargers was memorable for all the wrong reasons. The Bengals got crushed, 31–14. The hometown crowd grew frustrated with Anderson, and chants of "We want Jack!" broke out during various points in the game. Some fans even cheered when Anderson left the game in the third quarter with a knee injury. (He didn't return but was able to play the following week.) Anderson called the fans that cheered his injury "jerks" after the game.

Cincinnati didn't have a Pro Bowl player for a third straight season. But second-year tight end Dan Ross was a bright spot, hauling in a team-leading 56 receptions for 724 yards and four touchdowns.

Despite any injury concerns, Munoz played in all 16 games as a rookie.

Schedule

OPPONENT	SCORE	RECORD
L Tampa Bay Buccaneers	12–17	0–1
L @ Miami Dolphins	16–17	0–2
W Pittsburgh Steelers	30–28	1–2
L Houston Oilers	10–13	1–3
L @ Green Bay Packers	9–14	1–4
W @ Pittsburgh Steelers	17–16	2–4
W Minnesota Vikings	14–0	3–4
L @ Houston Oilers	3–23	3–5
L San Diego Chargers	14–31	3–6
L @ Oakland Raiders	17–28	3–7
L Buffalo Bills	0–14	3–8
L @ Cleveland Browns	7–31	3–9
W @ Kansas City Chiefs	20–6	4–9
W Baltimore Colts	34–33	5–9
W @ Chicago Bears (OT)	17–14	6–9
L Cleveland Browns	24–27	6–10

Season Leaders

CATEGORY	TOTAL	PLAYER
Passing Yards	1,778	Ken Anderson
Rushing Yards	747	Pete Johnson
Receiving Yards	724	Dan Ross
Receptions	56	Dan Ross
Interceptions	7	Louis Breeden
Sacks	12	Eddie Edwards
Points	48	Ian Sunter

Key Additions:
Jim Breech (free agent),
Anthony Munoz (draft)

Starting Lineup

Isaac Curtis  Ken Riley

Charles Alexander RB

Anthony Munoz LT   Reggie Williams

Ross Browner

Glenn Bujnoch  LG   Glenn Cameron   SS Greg Bright

Ken Anderson QB

Blair Bush C   Wilson Whitley   Jim LeClair    FS Dick Jauron

Max Montoya RG   Eddie Edwards

Pete Johnson RB

Mike Wilson RT   Tom Dinkel

Dan Ross TE

K Ian Sunter
KR Cleo Montgomery
P Pat McInally
PR Cleo Montgomery

Don Bass  WR   CB Ray Griffin

Bengals Trivia

Cincinnati's all-time best player, Anthony Munoz was elected to the hall of fame in 1998.

The Bengals
Draft Munoz

1980

Pro Bowl Selections

• None

12-4
First in AFC Central / AFC Champions

The Bengals' 1981 season started with a quarterback competition. Ken Anderson beat out Jack Thompson for the starting job, and he went on to become the first player in team history to win the league's MVP award.

Behind Anderson, the Bengals won the AFC Central for the first time since 1973. The offense finished third in the NFL in points scored (421). Combined with a stingy defense led by Reggie Williams, Ross Browner, and Eddie Edwards, Cincinnati had legitimate Super Bowl aspirations.

In the postseason, the Bengals beat the Buffalo Bills, 28–21, in the Divisional Round. Anderson found rookie sensation Cris Collinsworth for a 16-yard touchdown in the fourth quarter to clinch the team's first-ever playoff win.

The San Diego Chargers visited Riverfront Stadium the following week for the AFC Championship Game. A Super Bowl appearance was on the line, but the game was remembered for its bone-chilling temperatures that players and fans had to endure. The temperature was -9° for the contest, and the wind chill felt like -59°—with gusts up to 35 miles per hour.

The Bengals' offensive and defensive linemen played in short sleeves to prove they weren't bothered by the cold. The Chargers, however, were. They struggled, particularly on offense, and turned the ball over four times. The Bengals sent 46,302 fans home happy, as they crushed the Chargers, 27–7, in what came to be known as the "Freezer Bowl."

Super Bowl XVI didn't go the way Cincinnati hoped. (See page 44.) They fell to the San Francisco 49ers, 26–21. Yet it was a successful season by any measure. Collinsworth quickly became one of the team's most popular players. Tight end Dan Ross set a club record with 71 receptions. Running back Pete Johnson rushed for a career-high 1,077 yards.

Pro Bowl Selections

- Ken Anderson (QB)
- Cris Collinsworth (WR)
- Pete Johnson (RB)
- Pat McInally (P)
- Anthony Munoz (OT)

Schedule

	OPPONENT	SCORE	RECORD
W	Seattle Seahawks	27–21	1–0
W	@ New York Jets	31–30	2–0
L	Cleveland Browns	17–20	2–1
W	Buffalo Bills (OT)	27–24	3–1
L	@ Houston Oilers	10–17	3–2
W	@ Baltimore Colts	41–19	4–2
W	Pittsburgh Steelers	34–7	5–2
L	@ New Orleans Saints	7–17	5–3
W	Houston Oilers	34–21	6–3
W	@ San Diego Chargers	40–17	7–3
W	Los Angeles Rams	24–10	8–3
W	Denver Broncos	38–21	9–3
W	@ Cleveland Browns	41–21	10–3
L	San Francisco 49ers	3–21	10–4
W	@ Pittsburgh Steelers	17–10	11–4
W	@ Atlanta Falcons	30–28	12–4
W	*Buffalo Bills*	*28–21*	*1–0*
W	*San Diego Chargers*	*27–7*	*2–0*
L	*San Francisco 49ers (Pontiac, MI)*	*21–26*	*2–1*

Season Leaders

CATEGORY	TOTAL	PLAYER
Passing Yards	3,754	Ken Anderson
Rushing Yards	1,077	Pete Johnson
Receiving Yards	1,009	Cris Collinsworth
Receptions	71	Dan Ross
Interceptions	5	Ken Riley
Sacks	11	Reggie Williams
Points	115	Jim Breech

Key Additions:
Cris Collinsworth (draft)

Cris Collinsworth had 700+ yards receiving in six of eight NFL seasons.

Starting Lineup

OFFENSE	POSITION
Ken Anderson	QB
Charles Alexander	RB
Pete Johnson	RB
Isaac Curtis	WR
Cris Collinsworth	WR
Dan Ross	TE
Anthony Munoz	LT
Dave Lapham	LG
Blair Bush	C
Max Montoya	RG
Mike Wilson	RT

DEFENSE	POSITION
Eddie Edwards	DE
Wilson Whitley	DT
Ross Browner	DE
Bo Harris	OLB
Jim LeClair	MLB
Glenn Cameron	MLB
Reggie Williams	OLB
Louis Breeden	CB
Ken Riley	CB
Bobby Kemp	SS
Bryan Hicks	FS

SPECIAL TEAMS	POSITION
Jim Breech	K
David Verser	KR
Pat McInally	P
Mike Fuller	PR

Super Season

The 1981 season is one of the most memorable in team history. Not only did Cincinnati win their first division title since 1973, but they finished with a franchise-record 12 wins. That success carried into the postseason, as Cincinnati beat Buffalo and San Diego to be crowned AFC champions for the first time in franchise history and advanced to Super Bowl XVI.

The roster was stacked with a mix of talent on offense and defense. Quarterback Ken Anderson became the first Bengals player to win the NFL MVP Award. Running back Pete Johnson was a Pro Bowler. A young wide receiver named Cris Collinsworth finished second in Offensive Rookie of the Year voting. Meanwhile, Louis Breeden, Ross Browner, Eddie Edwards, Ken Riley, and Reggie Williams were significant contributors on defense. The Bengals also got high-end special teams play with punter Pat McInally being named an All-Pro and Jim Breech establishing himself as the Bengals' long-term answer at kicker.

Despite all of that, the Bengals got off to a nightmarish start in Super Bowl XVI against the San Francisco 49ers. Cincinnati turned over the ball three times in the first half. They trailed the 49ers 20–0 after two quarters, the largest halftime deficit in Super Bowl history at the time.

Anderson and the Bengals rallied in the second half, cutting San Francisco's lead to 20–14 early in the fourth quarter. However, the 49ers responded with two field goals to take a double-digit lead.

Tight end Dan Ross scored a touchdown with 16 seconds remaining to make the score look more respectable, but San Francisco recovered the ensuing onside kick to secure a 26–21 victory.

After a stellar 1,077-yard season in 1981, Pete Johnson was held to 36 yards rushing in Super Bowl XVI.

7–2
First in AFC Central

The Bengals hoped to rebound from their heartbreaking Super Bowl loss. Most of their key players returned for what ended up being a strike-shortened season.

Cincinnati began 1–1, but the NFL Players Association went on strike following Week 2. The strike, which largely revolved around revenue sharing, lasted 57 days. All games from Week 3 to Week 9 were canceled.

The Bengals resumed play on November 21. They won four straight games and looked like one of the NFL's best teams. Ken Riley tied his career high with three interceptions in a game against the Los Angeles Raiders, including one that he returned 56 yards for a touchdown.

Cincinnati lost to the San Diego Chargers on Monday Night Football in a 50–34 shootout. Ken Anderson completed 40 passes, which set a new team record. The Bengals shook off that December loss and won two games to end the regular season. They captured back-to-back division titles for the first time in team history.

The playoffs were expanded to 16 teams due to the strike. The third-seeded Bengals welcomed the sixth-seeded New York Jets to town for what became one of the franchise's worst postseason losses. Cincinnati built a 14–3 first-quarter lead, but New York scored 20 unanswered points and cruised to a 44–17 win—the most points ever allowed by a Bengals team in the postseason.

Anderson led the NFL in multiple passing categories, including completions (218) and completion percentage (70.6), which set a franchise record. Anthony Munoz was an All-Pro for a second straight season. Louis Breeden was also named to the All-Pro team.

Pro Bowl Selections

- Ken Anderson (QB)
- Cris Collinsworth (WR)
- Anthony Munoz (OT)
- Dan Ross (TE)

Schedule

	OPPONENT	SCORE	RECORD
W	Houston Oilers	27–6	1–0
L	@ Pittsburgh Steelers (OT)	20–26	1–1
	Did Not Play		
	Did Not Play		
	Did Not Play		
	Did Not Play		
	Did Not Play		
	Did Not Play		
	Did Not Play		
W	@ Philadelphia Eagles	18–14	2–1
W	Los Angeles Raiders	31–17	3–1
W	@ Baltimore Colts	20–17	4–1
W	Cleveland Browns	23–10	5–1
L	@ San Diego Chargers	34–50	5–2
W	Seattle Seahawks	24–10	6–2
W	@ Houston Oilers	35–27	7–2
L	*New York Jets*	17–44	0–1

Season Leaders

CATEGORY	TOTAL	PLAYER
Passing Yards	2,495	Ken Anderson
Rushing Yards	622	Pete Johnson
Receiving Yards	700	Cris Collinsworth
Receptions	49	Cris Collinsworth
Interceptions	5	Ken Riley
Sacks	6	Eddie Edwards
Points	67	Jim Breech

Key Additions:
Rodney Holman (draft)

Dan Ross was named to his only Pro Bowl in 1982.

Starting Lineup

OFFENSE	POSITION
Ken Anderson	QB
Charles Alexander	RB
Pete Johnson	RB
Isaac Curtis	WR
Cris Collinsworth	WR
Dan Ross	TE
Anthony Munoz	LT
Dave Lapham	LG
Blair Bush	C
Max Montoya	RG
Mike Wilson	RT

DEFENSE	POSITION
Eddie Edwards	DE
Wilson Whitley	DT
Ross Browner	DE
Bo Harris	OLB
Jim LeClair	MLB
Glenn Cameron	MLB
Reggie Williams	OLB
Louis Breeden	CB
Ken Riley	CB
Bobby Kemp	SS
Bryan Hicks	FS

SPECIAL TEAMS	POSITION
Jim Breech	K
David Verser	KR
Pat McInally	P
Mike Fuller	PR

7–9
Third in AFC Central

The 1983 season was a fall to mediocrity for the Bengals. After posting a 19–6 record during the previous two seasons and winning back-to-back division titles—as well as an AFC championship—the Bengals' run came to an end.

Cincinnati started the season 1–6 and failed to make the playoffs. Ken Anderson missed three games with a neck injury, which he suffered against the Pittsburgh Steelers after defensive end Keith Gary infamously twisted Anderson's helmet while sacking him.

The Bengals rallied, winning three straight games, but it wasn't enough. Cincinnati finished 7–9. The defense shined, however. They allowed 270.4 yards per game, which ranked first in the NFL—the only time Cincinnati ever finished first in total defense.

Head coach Forrest Gregg opted to resign after the season. He posted a 32–25 record in four seasons, which included a Super Bowl appearance. Gregg went on to coach the Green Bay Packers for four seasons. In his place, the Bengals hired Indiana University head coach Sam Wyche to lead the team into a new era of Cincinnati football. Wyche had played quarterback in the NFL for seven seasons, including three with the Bengals (1968–1970).

Legendary cornerback Ken Riley was named to the Pro Bowl in his final season. He retired after 15 years in the league. Riley finished his career with 65 interceptions, the fifth most in NFL history. He was later named to the Bengals Ring of Honor, and he became the second Bengals player to be voted into the Pro Football Hall of Fame in 2023, joining Anthony Munoz.

Offensive lineman Dave Lapham also left the team after the 1983 season. He joined the United States Football League (USFL) and spent two years playing for the New Jersey Generals.

Pro Bowl Selections

- Cris Collinsworth (WR)
- Anthony Munoz (OT)

Schedule

OPPONENT	SCORE	RECORD
L Los Angeles Raiders	10–20	0–1
L Buffalo Bills	6–10	0–2
L @ Cleveland Browns	7–17	0–3
W @ Tampa Bay Buccaneers	23–17	1–3
L Baltimore Colts	31–34	1–4
L Pittsburgh Steelers	14–24	1–5
L @ Denver Broncos	17–24	1–6
W Cleveland Browns	28–21	2–6
W Green Bay Packers	34–14	3–6
W @ Houston Oilers	55–14	4–6
L @ Kansas City Chiefs	15–20	4–7
W Houston Oilers	38–10	5–7
L @ Miami Dolphins	14–38	5–8
W @ Pittsburgh Steelers	23–10	6–8
W Detroit Lions	17–9	7–8
L @ Minnesota Vikings	14–20	7–9

Season Leaders

CATEGORY	TOTAL	PLAYER
Passing Yards	2,333	Ken Anderson
Rushing Yards	763	Pete Johnson
Receiving Yards	1,130	Cris Collinsworth
Receptions	66	Cris Collinsworth
Interceptions	8	Ken Riley
Sacks	13	Eddie Edwards
Points	87	Jim Breech

Key Additions:
Tim Krumrie (draft),
Dave Rimington (draft)

Starting Lineup

OFFENSE	POSITION
Ken Anderson	QB
Charles Alexander	RB
Pete Johnson	RB
Isaac Curtis	WR
Cris Collinsworth	WR
Dan Ross	TE
Anthony Munoz	LT
Dave Lapham	LG
Dave Rimington	C
Max Montoya	RG
Mike Wilson	RT

DEFENSE	POSITION
Eddie Edwards	DE
Jerry Boyarsky	DT
Ross Browner	DE
Tom Dinkel	OLB
Jim LeClair	MLB
Glenn Cameron	MLB
Reggie Williams	OLB
Louis Breeden	CB
Ken Riley	CB
Bobby Kemp	SS
Robert Jackson	FS

SPECIAL TEAMS	POSITION
Jim Breech	K
John Simmons	KR
Pat McInally	P
John Simmons/Mike Martin	PR

"I was always taught humility. Let your works speak for you."

—Ken Riley

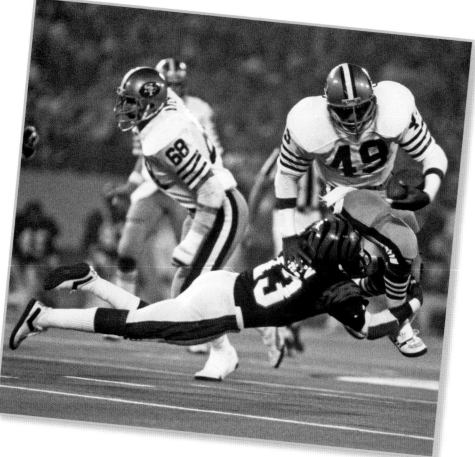

Ken Riley started 202 games at cornerback in his hall-of-fame career.

8–8
Second in AFC Central

The Sam Wyche era began with plenty of twists and turns on offense. The new head coach wanted to catch opposing defenses off guard. He experimented with different tactics, including having 15 to 20 players huddle around him during timeouts. Wyche would call a play, and as soon as the ball was put in play, 11 players would sprint to the line of scrimmage. (This was quickly banned by the NFL.)

Wyche's system continued to evolve into something he called the "sugar huddle." Instead of spending 20 seconds in the huddle, the Bengals would spend five seconds or less in the huddle because it was "short and sweet." Yet, despite Wyche's innovations, the Bengals got off to a slow start, losing their first five games.

With star quarterback Ken Anderson nearing the end of his career, Wyche was searching for the right signal-caller to lead his team into the future. Anderson started nine games, and veteran Turk Schonert started three, while promising rookie Boomer Esiason made four starts.

Once the team got the hang of Wyche's system, the Bengals went 8–3 down the stretch. This included four straight wins to end the season. Cincinnati averaged 32.8 points per game during those final four contests, which gave the team plenty of confidence. They nearly made the playoffs, finishing just one game behind the Pittsburgh Steelers in the AFC Central.

The Bengals' biggest win came before the season even started, when they traded fullback Pete Johnson to the Chargers in exchange for running back James Brooks. Johnson had been a valuable member of the team, but he was nearing the end of his career. Brooks, on the other hand, would become a core piece of the franchise for the next eight seasons and is arguably the greatest running back in team history.

Longtime wide receiver Isaac Curtis retired prior to the 1985 season. He finished his career with 416 receptions for 7,101 yards and 53 touchdowns. He left the game as Cincinnati's all-time leader in receiving yards and receiving touchdowns.

Schedule

OPPONENT	SCORE	RECORD
L @ Denver Broncos	17–20	0–1
L Kansas City Chiefs	22–27	0–2
L @ New York Jets	23–43	0–3
L Los Angeles Rams	14–24	0–4
L @ Pittsburgh Steelers	17–38	0–5
W Houston Oilers	13–3	1–5
L @ New England Patriots	14–20	1–6
W Cleveland Browns	12–9	2–6
W @ Houston Oilers	31–13	3–6
L @ San Francisco 49ers	17–23	3–7
W Pittsburgh Steelers	22–20	4–7
L Seattle Seahawks	6–26	4–8
W Atlanta Falcons	35–14	5–8
W @ Cleveland Browns (OT)	20–17	6–8
W @ New Orleans Saints	24–21	7–8
W Buffalo Bills	52–21	8–8

Season Leaders

CATEGORY	TOTAL	PLAYER
Passing Yards	2,107	Ken Anderson
Rushing Yards	623	Larry Kinnebrew
Receiving Yards	989	Cris Collinsworth
Receptions	64	Cris Collinsworth
Interceptions	4	Breeden, Jackson, Kemp
Sacks	9	E. Edwards, R. Williams
Points	103	Jim Breech

Key Additions:
James Brooks (trade), Boomer Esiason (draft), Bruce Kozerski (draft)

Starting Lineup

Isaac Curtis (WR) Ray Horton (CB)

Anthony Munoz (LT)

Charles Alexander (RB)

Brian Blados (LG) Ross Browner (DE)

Ken Anderson (QB)

Dave Rimington (C) Tim Krumrie (NT)

James Brooks (RB)

Max Montoya (RG) Eddie Edwards (DE)

Mike Wilson (RT)

M.L. Harris (TE)

Cris Collinsworth (WR) Louis Breeden (CB)

Reggie Williams (LB)

Glenn Cameron (LB) Bobby Kemp (SS)

Ron Simpkins (LB) Robert Jackson (FS)

Jeff Schuh (LB)

K   Jim Breech
KR Stanford Jennings
P   Pat McInally
PR Mike Martin

Bengals Trivia

Isaac Curtis holds the franchise record for career average yards per reception (17.1).

Pro Bowl Selections

• Anthony Munoz (OT)

The Sam Wyche Era Begins

1984

51

7–9
Second in AFC Central

The Bengals offense made another step forward under Sam Wyche in 1985. Second-year quarterback Boomer Esiason took the reins from Ken Anderson in Week 3. He started 14 games and threw for 3,443 yards and 27 touchdowns.

Cincinnati got off to another slow start, dropping their first three games, despite averaging more than 30 points per game. They clawed their way to .500 after beating the Cleveland Browns in Week 10 to improve to 5–5.

The team kept their playoff hopes alive after splitting the next four games to get to 7–7. But instead of rallying toward the postseason, the Bengals blew a 17-point lead and fell to Washington and then lost to New England in the final week. They missed the playoffs for a third straight season.

Cincinnati's defense allowed 437 points, the third-worst in the NFL. But defensive tackle Tim Krumrie played well, with 96 tackles and 3.5 sacks.

Rookie wide receiver Eddie Brown took the league by storm, hauling in 53 passes for 942 yards and eight touchdowns. He became the first player in team history to win the Associated Press Offensive Rookie of the Year Award. Brown was the perfect complement to Cris Collinsworth, who led the team with 65 catches for 1,125 yards and five scores.

Running back James Brooks emerged as a star in his second season in Cincinnati, finishing with a team-leading 929 yards rushing and seven touchdowns on 4.8 yards per carry. He was also second on the team in receptions (55), gained 576 yards receiving, and caught five touchdowns.

The Bengals didn't make the playoffs, but they did find their franchise quarterback. With proven players like Collinsworth and Anthony Munoz (who was named a first-team All-Pro for the fourth time), as well as young weapons in Brooks and Brown, the organization held plenty of optimism about the future.

Pro Bowl Selections

- Anthony Munoz (OT)

Schedule

	OPPONENT	SCORE	RECORD
L	Seattle Seahawks	24–28	0–1
L	@ Saint Louis Cardinals	27–41	0–2
L	San Diego Chargers	41–44	0–3
W	@ Pittsburgh Steelers	37–24	1–3
L	New York Jets	20–29	1–4
W	New York Giants	35–30	2–4
L	@ Houston Oilers	27–44	2–5
W	Pittsburgh Steelers	26–21	3–5
W	@ Buffalo Bills	23–17	4–5
W	Cleveland Browns	27–10	5–5
L	@ Los Angeles Raiders	6–13	5–6
L	@ Cleveland Browns	6–24	5–7
W	Houston Oilers	45–27	6–7
W	Dallas Cowboys	50–24	7–7
L	@ Washington	24–27	7–8
L	@ New England Patriots	23–34	7–9

Season Leaders

CATEGORY	TOTAL	PLAYER
Passing Yards	3,443	Boomer Esiason
Rushing Yards	929	James Brooks
Receiving Yards	1,125	Cris Collinsworth
Receptions	65	Cris Collinsworth
Interceptions	7	James Griffin
Sacks	9	Ross Browner
Points	120	Jim Breech

Key Additions:
Eddie Brown (draft), Joe Walter (draft), Carl Zander (draft)

Louis Breeden spent 10 seasons with the Bengals and started 115 games.

Starting Lineup

OFFENSE	POSITION
Boomer Esiason	QB
Larry Kinnebrew	RB
James Brooks	RB
Eddie Brown	WR
Cris Collinsworth	WR
Rodney Holman	TE
Anthony Munoz	LT
Brian Blados	LG
Dave Rimington	C
Max Montoya	RG
Mike Wilson	RT

DEFENSE	POSITION
Eddie Edwards	DE
Tim Krumrie	DT
Ross Browner	DE
Jeff Schuh	OLB
Ron Simpkins	MLB
Glenn Cameron	MLB
Reggie Williams	OLB
Louis Breeden	CB
Ray Horton	CB
Bobby Kemp	SS
James Griffin	FS

SPECIAL TEAMS	POSITION
Jim Breech	K
Mike Martin	KR
Pat McInally	P
Mike Martin	PR

10–6
Second in AFC Central

In 1986, the Bengals posted their first winning record since 1982. Head coach Sam Wyche's offense took off in Boomer Esiason's first full season as the starting quarterback. Cincinnati began 5–2 and topped the 30-point mark in four of their first seven games.

The hot start on offense continued for much of the year, as Esiason threw for a club record 3,959 yards. The Bengals averaged 25.6 points per game, the third most in the NFL. However, the defense struggled. They allowed 394 points, which ranked 23rd overall. With Esiason throwing 17 interceptions, it was easy to see why opposing offenses fared so well.

Nevertheless, the Bengals entered Week 15 with a 9–5 record and a home matchup against the Cleveland Browns, with the AFC Central Division title on the line. Cincinnati had already beaten Cleveland in Week 3, but the rematch was much different. The Bengals offense struggled, and the Browns never trailed in their 34–3 victory. Cleveland clinched the division with the win, ending Cincinnati's chances of making the postseason.

The Bengals beat the Jets, 52–21, in Week 16 to finish 10–6. They joined the 1976 club (10–4) as the only Bengals teams to win 10 or more games and not qualify for the postseason.

Running back James Brooks made the Pro Bowl for the first time. He led the NFL with 5.3 yards per carry and set a single-season Bengals record for yards from scrimmage with 1,773. Linebacker Reggie Williams won the NFL Man of the Year award after making a major impact on and off the field.

The 1986 campaign was also Ken Anderson's final season in the NFL. He spent 16 seasons in Cincinnati, the longest tenure in team history. He was named league MVP in 1981, helped Cincinnati reach Super Bowl XVI, and was inducted into the Bengals Ring of Honor in 2021.

Pro Bowl Selections

- James Brooks (RB)
- Boomer Esiason (QB)
- Max Montoya (G)
- Anthony Munoz (OT)

Schedule

OPPONENT	SCORE	RECORD
L @ Kansas City Chiefs	14–24	0–1
W Buffalo Bills (OT)	36–33	1–1
W @ Cleveland Browns	30–13	2–1
L Chicago Bears	7–44	2–2
W @ Green Bay Packers	34–28	3–2
W Pittsburgh Steelers	24–22	4–2
W Houston Oilers	31–28	5–2
L @ Pittsburgh Steelers	9–30	5–3
W @ Detroit Lions	24–17	6–3
L @ Houston Oilers	28–32	6–4
W Seattle Seahawks	34–7	7–4
W Minnesota Vikings	24–20	8–4
L @ Denver Broncos	28–34	8–5
W @ New England Patriots	31–7	9–5
L Cleveland Browns	3–34	9–6
W New York Jets	52–21	10–6

Season Leaders

CATEGORY	TOTAL	PLAYER
Passing Yards	3,959	Boomer Esiason
Rushing Yards	1,087	James Brooks
Receiving Yards	1,024	Cris Collinsworth
Receptions	62	Cris Collinsworth
Interceptions	7	Louis Breeden
Sacks	9	Emanuel King
Points	101	Jim Breech

Key Additions:
David Fulcher (draft), Tim McGee (draft)

Starting Lineup

OFFENSE	POSITION
Boomer Esiason	QB
Larry Kinnebrew	RB
James Brooks	RB
Eddie Brown	WR
Cris Collinsworth	WR
Rodney Holman	TE
Anthony Munoz	LT
Bruce Kozerski	LG
Dave Rimington	C
Max Montoya	RG
Brian Blados	RT

DEFENSE	POSITION
Eddie Edwards	DE
Tim Krumrie	DT
Ross Browner	DE
Emanuel King	OLB
Carl Zander	MLB
Leo Barker	MLB
Reggie Williams	OLB
Louis Breeden	CB
Lewis Billups	CB
David Fulcher	SS
Bobby Kemp	FS

SPECIAL TEAMS	POSITION
Jim Breech	K
Tim McGee	KR
Jeff Hayes	P
Mike Martin	PR

Max Montoya was elected to his first of four Pro Bowls in 1986.

"We really believed that if we just went in and played our style of football that we would win".

—Ken Anderson

4–11
Fourth in AFC Central

After posting a 10–6 record in 1986, most expected Cincinnati to take another step forward. Instead, the players' union went on strike early in the season, which threw a wrench in Cincinnati's chances of making a playoff run.

The Bengals started the season 1–1, which included a heartbreaking one-point loss to the San Francisco 49ers. With a six-point lead and just six seconds remaining, head coach Sam Wyche opted to go for it on fourth down from his own 30-yard line. He called a run to James Brooks in hopes of eating up the clock, but the play was stopped in the backfield with two seconds remaining. With one last chance, San Francisco's hall-of-fame duo seized it: Quarterback Joe Montana found wide receiver Jerry Rice for a 25-yard touchdown—and a 27–26 win.

The NFL Players Association went on strike following Week 2. Among the players' demands were an improved pension and the right to free agency. Week 3 games were canceled, but the owners quickly pivoted and used replacement players beginning in Week 4. The Bengals were 1–2 in "replacement games."

NFL veterans agreed to return to work prior to Week 7. The regular players were back on the field but struggled to find their winning ways. Cincinnati dropped three games in a row and went 2–5 down the stretch to finish with just four wins for the fifth time in franchise history.

Defensive tackle Tim Krumrie finished with 88 tackles and three sacks. He was named to his first Pro Bowl.

The Bengals opted to keep head coach Sam Wyche after the 1987 season. He had posted a 29–33 record in his first four seasons and was entering the final year of his contract with the team.

Pro Bowl Selections

- Anthony Munoz (OT)
- Tim Krumrie (DT)

Schedule

	OPPONENT	SCORE	RECORD
W	@ Indianapolis Colts	23–21	1–0
L	San Francisco 49ers	26–27	1–1
	Did Not Play		
L	San Diego Chargers	9–10	1–2
W	@ Seattle Seahawks	17–10	2–2
L	Cleveland Browns	0–34	2–3
L	@ Pittsburgh Steelers	20–23	2–4
L	Houston Oilers	29–31	2–5
L	Miami Dolphins	14–20	2–6
W	@ Atlanta Falcons	16–10	3–6
L	Pittsburgh Steelers	16–30	3–7
L	@ New York Jets	20–27	3–8
W	Kansas City Chiefs (OT)	30–27	4–8
L	@ Cleveland Browns	24–38	4–9
L	New Orleans Saints	24–41	4–10
L	@ Houston Oilers	17–21	4–11

Season Leaders

CATEGORY	TOTAL	PLAYER
Passing Yards	3,321	Boomer Esiason
Rushing Yards	570	Larry Kinnebrew
Receiving Yards	44	Eddie Brown
Receptions	608	Eddie Brown
Interceptions	3	D. Fulcher, R. Jackson
Sacks	6	Reggie Williams
Points	97	Jim Breech

Key Additions:
Eric Thomas (draft),
Solomon Wilcots (draft)

Jim Breech is the Bengals' all-time leading scorer with 1,151 points.

Starting Lineup

OFFENSE	POSITION
Boomer Esiason	QB
Larry Kinnebrew	RB
James Brooks	RB
Eddie Brown	WR
Cris Collinsworth	WR
Rodney Holman	TE
Anthony Munoz	LT
Bruce Reimers	LG
Dave Rimington	C
Max Montoya	RG
Joe Walter	RT

DEFENSE	POSITION
Eddie Edwards	DE
Tim Krumrie	DT
Jim Skow	DE
Emanuel King	OLB
Carl Zander	MLB
Joe Kelly	MLB
Reggie Williams	OLB
Ray Horton	CB
Lewis Billups	CB
David Fulcher	SS
Robert Jackson	FS

SPECIAL TEAMS	POSITION
Jim Breech	K
Barney Bussey	KR
Scott Fulhage	P
Mike Martin	PR

12–4
First in AFC Central / AFC Champions

Sam Wyche's offensive system peaked in 1988. The Bengals started 6–0 and established themselves as one of the NFL's best teams. Boomer Esiason led the way, and Eddie Brown had his best season, hauling in 53 receptions for 1,273 yards and nine touchdowns.

James Brooks paced the ground attack, but the Bengals found a perfect one-two punch when they chose Ickey Woods in the second round of the 1988 NFL Draft. Woods led the NFL with 5.3 yards per carry and scored 15 touchdowns. His famous "Ickey Shuffle" touchdown dance became one of the most popular celebrations in sports history.

Cincinnati finished 12–4 and earned the top seed in the AFC playoffs. The team hosted the Seattle Seahawks at Riverfront Stadium in the Divisional Round. The Bengals built a 21–0 halftime lead behind their hurry-up, no-huddle offense. Seattle scored two touchdowns late in the game, but Cincinnati won, 21–13.

The NFL banned Cincinnati's no-huddle offense in the AFC Championship Game against the Buffalo Bills—just two hours before kickoff. It stirred up tremendous controversy, particularly with the timing of the rule change. But it ultimately didn't matter. The Bengals leaned on their rushing attack with a Super Bowl appearance on the line. Woods ran for 102 yards and a touchdown. Brooks added another score through the air, and Cincinnati never trailed in their 21–10 win over Buffalo.

The Bengals advanced to Super Bowl XXIII, where they met the same quarterback and the same team that had beaten them in Super Bowl XVI: Joe Montana and the San Francisco 49ers. It proved to be one of the most memorable games in NFL history. (See page 61.)

Pro Bowl Selections

- James Brooks (RB)
- Eddie Brown (WR)
- Boomer Esiason (QB)
- David Fulcher (S)
- Rodney Holman (TE)
- Tim Krumrie (DT)
- Max Montoya (G)
- Anthony Munoz (OT)

Schedule

OPPONENT	SCORE	RECORD
W Phoenix Cardinals	21–14	1–0
W @ Philadelphia Eagles	28–24	2–0
W @ Pittsburgh Steelers	17–12	3–0
W Cleveland Browns	24–17	4–0
W @ Los Angeles Raiders	45–21	5–0
W New York Jets	36–19	6–0
L @ New England Patriots	21–27	6–1
W Houston Oilers	44–21	7–1
L @ Cleveland Browns	16–23	7–2
W Pittsburgh Steelers	42–7	8–2
L @ Kansas City Chiefs	28–31	8–3
W @ Dallas Cowboys	38–24	9–3
W Buffalo Bills	35–21	10–3
W San Diego Chargers	27–10	11–3
L @ Houston Oilers	6–41	11–4
W Washington (OT)	20–17	12–4
W *Seattle Seahawks*	*21–13*	*1–0*
W *Buffalo Bills*	*21–10*	*2–0*
L *San Francisco 49ers (Miami, FL)*	*16–20*	*2–1*

Season Leaders

CATEGORY	TOTAL	PLAYER
Passing Yards	3,572	Boomer Esiason
Rushing Yards	1,066	Ickey Woods
Receiving Yards	44	Eddie Brown
Receptions	1,273	Eddie Brown
Interceptions	7	Eric Thomas
Sacks	9.5	Jim Skow
Points	90	Ickey Woods

Key Additions:
Lee Johnson (free agent), Ickey Woods (draft)

Starting Lineup

OFFENSE	POSITION	DEFENSE	POSITION
Boomer Esiason	QB	Skip McClendon	DE
Ickey Woods	RB	Tim Krumrie	DT
James Brooks	RB	Jim Skow	DE
Eddie Brown	WR	Leon White	OLB
Tim McGee	WR	Carl Zander	MLB
Rodney Holman	TE	Joe Kelly	MLB
Anthony Munoz	LT	Reggie Williams	OLB
Bruce Reimers	LG	Lewis Billups	CB
Bruce Kozerski	C	Eric Thomas	CB
Max Montoya	RG	David Fulcher	SS
Joe Walter	RT	Solomon Wilcots	FS

SPECIAL TEAMS	POSITION
Jim Breech	K
Stanford Jennings	KR
Scott Fulhage	P
Ira Hillary	PR

James Brooks was an elite running back in the late 1980s, averaging over five yards per carry.

A Game for the Ages

The 1980s were the most successful decade in Bengals history. After falling short in Super Bowl XVI, Cincinnati made another run to the Big Game seven years later, this time with Boomer Esiason under center.

Despite a controversial ban by the league of Cincinnati's no-huddle offense—an important part of their offensive strategy—the Bengals defeated the Buffalo Bills to advance to Super Bowl XXIII. That ban of the no-huddle offense lasted just one game; Esiason and the offense would be allowed to run it in the Super Bowl.

The battle against the San Francisco 49ers (again) and quarterback Joe Montana (again) became one of the greatest games in Super Bowl history. Unfortunately, Cincinnati's star defensive tackle Tim Krumrie suffered a gruesome broken leg in the first quarter. Still, the Bengals defense played well.

The game's first touchdown came late in the third quarter when Stanford Jennings returned a kickoff 93 yards to give Cincinnati a 13–6 advantage. The 49ers answered with a Montana connection to Jerry Rice for a 14-yard score, tying the game.

Both defenses held until Jim Breech kicked a 40-yard field goal with 3:20 left in the game, giving Cincinnati a 16–13 lead.

But there's a reason Montana is still discussed as arguably the best quarterback in NFL history. He calmly led the 49ers on an 11-play, 92-yard drive that ended with John Taylor's game-winning 10-yard touchdown catch with just 34 seconds remaining. San Francisco took their first and only lead of the game, but it was enough to break the hearts of Bengals fans everywhere.

The Bengals offense featured six Pro Bowl players, including Ickey Woods (30) and Rodney Holman (82).

1989

The defending AFC champions were hoping to repeat in 1989 after coming up just short in Super Bowl XXIII. They released wide receiver Cris Collinsworth during final preseason cuts. The three-time Pro Bowl player finished his career with 6,698 yards and 36 touchdowns.

On the field, the Bengals offense didn't miss a beat early in the season. They started 4–1, which included a 41–10 win over the Pittsburgh Steelers. However, Cincinnati lost four of their next five games and never got more than a game above .500 for the rest of the season.

It was a disappointing campaign for head coach Sam Wyche, but he did deliver one of the most memorable moments in team history. After some questionable officiating during a Week 14 home game against the Seattle Seahawks, Bengals fans started throwing snowballs onto the field. Wyche promptly grabbed a microphone and asked fans to stop, famously saying, "You don't live in Cleveland. You live in Cincinnati."

The Bengals entered their Week 16 matchup against the Minnesota Vikings with an 8–7 record. A win would secure a Wild Card berth in the playoffs. But Minnesota jumped to a 19–0 lead in the second quarter and never trailed in the game. Boomer Esiason tried to lead a comeback, throwing three touchdown passes, but the Vikings won, 29–21, to end the season.

Five of Cincinnati's losses were one-possession games. The Bengals ranked fourth in the NFL in total offense and fourth in points scored. On defense, they held opponents to 17.8 points per game, seventh best in the league.

Anthony Munoz was a first-team All-Pro for the eighth time. Safety David Fulcher was also a first-team All-Pro. Linebacker and Bengals legend Reggie Williams retired after the season.

Pro Bowl Selections

- James Brooks (RB)
- Boomer Esiason (QB)
- David Fulcher (S)
- Rodney Holman (TE)
- Max Montoya (G)
- Anthony Munoz (OT)

Schedule

	OPPONENT	SCORE	RECORD
L	@ Chicago Bears	14–17	0–1
W	Pittsburgh Steelers	41–10	1–1
W	Cleveland Browns	21–14	2–1
W	@ Kansas City Chiefs	21–17	3–1
W	@ Pittsburgh Steelers	26–16	4–1
L	Miami Dolphins	13–20	4–2
L	Indianapolis Colts	12–23	4–3
W	Tampa Bay Buccaneers	56–23	5–3
L	@ Los Angeles Raiders	7–28	5–4
L	@ Houston Oilers	24–26	5–5
W	Detroit Lions	42–7	6–5
L	@ Buffalo Bills	7–24	6–6
W	@ Cleveland Browns	21–0	7–6
L	Seattle Seahawks	17–24	7–7
W	Houston Oilers	61–7	8–7
L	Minnesota Vikings	21–29	8–8

Season Leaders

CATEGORY	TOTAL	PLAYER
Passing Yards	3,525	Boomer Esiason
Rushing Yards	1,239	James Brooks
Receiving Yards	65	Tim McGee
Receptions	1,211	Tim McGee
Interceptions	8	David Fulcher
Sacks	6	Jason Buck
Points	73	Jim Breech

Key Additions:
None

Starting Lineup

OFFENSE	POSITION
Boomer Esiason	QB
Eric Ball	RB
James Brooks	RB
Eddie Brown	WR
Tim McGee	WR
Rodney Holman	TE
Anthony Munoz	LT
Bruce Reimers	LG
Bruce Kozerski	C
Max Montoya	RG
Brian Blados	RT

DEFENSE	POSITION
Jim Skow	DE
Tim Krumrie	DT
Jason Buck	DE
Leon White	OLB
Carl Zander	MLB
Joe Kelly	MLB
Reggie Williams	OLB
Lewis Billups	CB
Eric Thomas	CB
David Fulcher	SS
Rickey Dixon	FS

SPECIAL TEAMS	POSITION
Jim Breech	K
Stanford Jennings	KR
Lee Johnson	P
Mike Martin	PR

"Don't try to be better than the other guy. Just try to be better than you were the day before. That's all you have to do."

—Sam Wyche

Reggie Williams (57) was a 14-year starter at linebacker for the Bengals.

All-1980s Offense

QUARTERBACK: The 1980s were the best decade in team history. Cincinnati won two AFC championships. Ken Anderson won the MVP in 1981 and led the Bengals to Super Bowl XVI, but **Boomer Esiason** (1984–1989) beats him out as our quarterback. Esiason threw for 18,350 yards and 126 touchdowns in 85 games. He was named MVP of the 1988 season and led Cincinnati to Super Bowl XXIII.

RUNNING BACKS: **James Brooks** (1984–1989) is arguably the best running back in franchise history and was certainly the most versatile. He ran for 4,872 yards and 30 scores on 4.9 yards per attempt. He also caught 231 passes for 2,395 yards and 21 touchdowns. He made three Pro Bowls in the 1980s. **Pete Johnson** (1980–1983) is Brooks' counterpart, which is ironic considering he was traded for Brooks prior to the 1984 season. Johnson helped the Bengals reach Super Bowl XVI in 1981. He totaled 3,209 rushing yards and 39 touchdowns in the early 1980s. Johnson gets the nod over Ickey Woods.

WIDE RECEIVERS: **Cris Collinsworth** (1981–1988) quickly established himself as one of the best receivers in team history after the Bengals took him in the second round of the 1981 NFL Draft. He was selected to the Pro Bowl in his first three seasons and averaged 16.1 yards per catch for his career. He topped the 1,000-yard mark four times and is fifth in team history with 6,698 receiving yards. **Eddie Brown** (1985–1989) beats out Isaac Curtis and Tim McGee for the second wide receiver spot. Brown had 260 receptions for 4,601 yards and 30 touchdowns in 75 games. He made the Pro Bowl in 1988 after posting a career-high 1,273 receiving yards.

TIGHT END: **Rodney Holman** (1982–1989) was a big part of the offense for most of the decade. He caught 221 passes for 3,022 yards and 25 scores in 117 games. He made back-to-back Pro Bowls in 1988 and 1989.

TACKLES: The offensive line was a team strength for most of the decade, led by **Anthony Munoz** (1980–1989). Not only is he a hall-of-fame player and considered the best player in team history, but many believe he's the NFL's greatest offensive lineman of all-time. Munoz was an eight-time All-Pro in the 1980s and made nine Pro Bowls. He also had four touchdown receptions. **Mike Wilson** (1980–1985) started 88 games at right tackle. He thrived playing alongside Max Montoya.

GUARDS: **Brian Blados** (1984–1989) narrowly edges out Dave Lapham at left guard. Blados made 53 starts and appeared in 88 games. **Max Montoya** (1980–1989) runs away with the right guard slot, making three Pro Bowls and 143 starts during the decade.

CENTER: **Bruce Kozerski** (1984–1989) is an easy choice at center. He started 50 games and appeared in 85 contests as a staple of the offensive line.

KICKER: **Jim Breech** (1980–1989) is considered the greatest kicker in team history. He kicked for the Bengals over almost the entire decade, which included clutch field goals during both postseason runs.

KICK RETURNER: **Stanford Jennings** (1984–1989) returned 107 kicks for 2,198 yards, including a 98-yard touchdown in 1988. He also scored a memorable touchdown on a 93-yard kick return in Super Bowl XXIII.

Statistics for the all-decade team are for the given decade only, unless otherwise noted.

All-1980s Defense

DEFENSIVE ENDS: Eddie Edwards (1980–1988) played in 128 games, racking up 69.5 sacks in the process. He finished his career with 84.5 sacks, the most in team history. **Ross Browner** (1980–1986) was another mainstay in the trenches, starting 96 games and finishing with 47.5 sacks over that span.

NOSE TACKLE: The Bengals defensive front was led by **Tim Krumrie** (1983–1989). He had 659 tackles and 20.5 sacks. He was also a first-team All-Pro in 1988. The trio of Krumrie, Edwards, and Browner was a problem for opposing quarterbacks during the mid-1980s.

LINEBACKERS: Reggie Williams (1980–1989) was a disruptive force at linebacker, finishing with 54 sacks and nine interceptions in 148 starts. **Jim LeClair** (1980–1983) started 52 games for the Bengals in the early 1980s, compiling 4.5 sacks and four takeaways. **Joe Kelly** (1986–1989) started 48 games and tallied 209 tackles with two interceptions. **Carl Zander** (1985–1989) also makes the cut with 67 starts. He had eight sacks, four fumble recoveries, and two interceptions over that span.

CORNERBACKS: Ken Riley (1980–1983) makes the team for a second straight decade. He had 21 interceptions and three touchdowns in 55 starts. He led the NFL with two interception returns for touchdowns in the 1983 season and was named a first-team All-Pro at 36 years old. **Louis Breeden** (1980–1987) appeared in 108 games, hauling in 30 interceptions and returning two for touchdowns, including a 102-yard return during the 1981 season. It stood as the franchise's longest play for 39 years.

SAFETIES: David Fulcher (1986–1989) started 59 games during the decade. A ball-hawking safety, he intercepted 20 passes, recovered six fumbles, and recorded 6.5 sacks. He was named to two Pro Bowls and was an All-Pro in 1989. **Bobby Kemp** (1981–1986) appeared in 83 games. He intercepted nine passes, recovered two fumbles, and added four sacks.

PUNTER: Pat McInally (1980–1985) led the NFL in yards per punt (45.4 yards) and was a first-team All-Pro in 1981. He played his entire 10-year career in Cincinnati and finished with an average of 41.9 yards per punt. Demonstrating his versatility, he also caught 57 passes for 808 yards and five touchdowns as a wide receiver.

PUNT RETURNER: Mike Martin (1983–1989) returned 140 punts for the Bengals, averaging 9.9 yards per return. He led the NFL with an average of 15.7 yards per return in 1984.

Eddie Brown finished with 800+ receiving yards in five of seven NFL seasons.

9–7
First in AFC Central

After missing the postseason in 1989, the Bengals rebounded by winning the AFC Central in 1990. It was their fourth division championship in 10 seasons.

Cincinnati started the year 5–2 after a Week 7 win over Cleveland. Their playoff chances took a major hit when they lost five of their next seven games. Instead of folding, they rallied in the final two weeks of the season. They crushed the Houston Oilers, 40–20, then they beat the Browns, 21–14, to clinch their second division title in three years.

Cincinnati hosted Houston in the Wild Card Round of the playoffs. The two teams split their two regular-season matchups, but this game wasn't close. The Bengals built a 34–0 lead and cruised to a 41–14 win.

They advanced to play the Raiders in Los Angeles. Early in the fourth quarter, Boomer Esiason found running back Stanford Jennings for an eight-yard touchdown reception to tie the game at 10. But Los Angeles responded with 10 straight points, and the Bengals didn't score again.

The loss marked an ending, of sorts, for Cincinnati Bengals football. The team's championship window had closed. Cincinnati's postseason victory over the Oilers would be their final playoff win for more than 30 years. This drought became known to some as "The Curse of Bo Jackson." The Raiders' superstar running back suffered a hip injury while getting tackled by linebacker Kevin Walker in the third quarter of their playoff matchup. Jackson never played in the NFL again, and the Bengals wouldn't qualify for the postseason again until the 2005 season.

Cincinnati finished seventh in points scored (360) in 1990. It was their third and final winning season under head coach Sam Wyche. Left tackle Anthony Munoz was named a first-team All-Pro for a ninth and final time.

Pro Bowl Selections

- James Brooks (RB)
- David Fulcher (S)
- Rodney Holman (TE)
- Anthony Munoz (OT)

Schedule

OPPONENT	SCORE	RECORD
W New York Jets	25–20	1–0
W @ San Diego Chargers	21–16	2–0
W New England Patriots	41–7	3–0
L @ Seattle Seahawks	16–31	3–1
W @ Los Angeles Rams (OT)	34–31	4–1
L @ Houston Oilers	17–48	4–2
W @ Cleveland Browns	34–13	5–2
L @ Atlanta Falcons	17–38	5–3
L New Orleans Saints	7–21	5–4
W Pittsburgh Steelers	27–3	6–4
L Indianapolis Colts	20–34	6–5
W @ Pittsburgh Steelers	16–12	7–5
L San Francisco 49ers (OT)	17–20	7–6
L @ Los Angeles Raiders	7–24	7–7
W Houston Oilers	40–20	8–7
W Cleveland Browns	21–14	9–7
W *Houston Oilers*	*41–14*	*1–0*
L *@ Los Angeles Raiders*	*10–20*	*1–1*

Season Leaders

CATEGORY	TOTAL	PLAYER
Passing Yards	3,031	Boomer Esiason
Rushing Yards	1,004	James Brooks
Receiving Yards	737	Tim McGee
Receptions	44	Eddie Brown
Interceptions	4	B. Bussey, D. Fulcher
Sacks	8	James Francis
Points	92	Jim Breech

Key Additions:
James Francis (draft), Harold Green (draft)

Starting Lineup

OFFENSE	POSITION
Boomer Esiason	QB
Harold Green	RB
James Brooks	RB
Eddie Brown	WR
Tim McGee	WR
Rodney Holman	TE
Anthony Munoz	LT
Bruce Reimers	LG
Bruce Kozerski	C
Ken Moyer	RG
Brian Blados	RT

DEFENSE	POSITION
Skip McClendon	DE
Tim Krumrie	DT
David Grant	DE
Leon White	OLB
Carl Zander	MLB
Kevin Walker	MLB
James Francis	OLB
Lewis Billups	CB
Carl Carter	CB
David Fulcher	SS
Solomon Wilcots	FS

SPECIAL TEAMS	POSITION
Jim Breech	K
Stanford Jennings	KR
Lee Johnson	P
Mitchell Price	PR

Tim Krumrie (69) was a tremendous run stopper in his 12-year career with the Bengals.

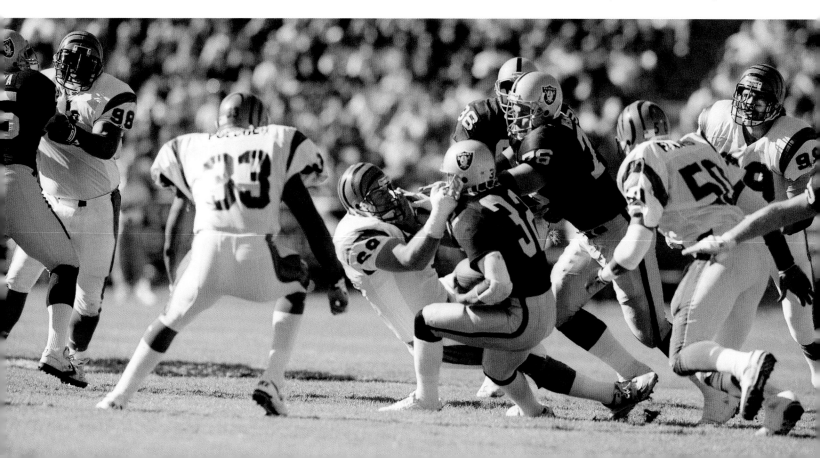

3–13
Fourth in AFC Central

Owner Paul Brown passed away on August 5, 1991, due to complications from pneumonia. Brown was the founder of the Bengals franchise, was their first head coach, and is a member of the Pro Football Hall of Fame. Mike Brown (Paul Brown's son) took over the team. He had served as his father's assistant prior to his father's death.

On the field, the 1991 season was forgettable. The Bengals started 0–8 with five losses by double digits. The team picked up their first win in Week 10, when they beat the Cleveland Browns, 23–21. Jim Breech kicked three field goals, including the game-winning 38-yarder in the fourth quarter. But the Bengals lost five of their last seven games to finish 3–13, their worst record in franchise history and just the second time they finished with less than four wins (3–11, 1968).

Boomer Esiason had his worst season since becoming a full-time starter in 1985. He threw more interceptions than touchdowns for the second time in his career with 13 touchdowns and 16 interceptions.

Following the disappointing season, Mike Brown fired head coach Sam Wyche. There was some debate about Wyche resigning rather than getting fired, but, either way, the team moved on without him. Before the season, Wyche had called out Brown publicly for releasing running back Stanford Jennings. Combined with a three-win season and other internal disagreements, it was no surprise that the duo decided to part ways. Wyche posted a 61–66 record over eight seasons, with three division titles and an AFC championship.

Brown promoted wide receivers coach Dave Shula to head coach. At 32 years old, Shula became one of the youngest head coaches in NFL history.

Anthony Munoz won the NFL Man of the Year award, joining Ken Anderson (1975) and Reggie Williams (1986) as Bengals who won the honor.

Pro Bowl Selections

• Anthony Munoz (OT)

Schedule

OPPONENT	SCORE	RECORD
L @ Denver Broncos	14–45	0–1
L Houston Oilers	7–30	0–2
L @ Cleveland Browns	13–14	0–3
L Washington	27–34	0–4
L Seattle Seahawks	7–13	0–5
L @ Dallas Cowboys	23–35	0–6
L @ Buffalo Bills	16–35	0–7
L @ Houston Oilers	3–35	0–8
W Cleveland Browns	23–21	1–8
L Pittsburgh Steelers (OT)	27–33	1–9
L @ Philadelphia Eagles	10–17	1–10
L Los Angeles Raiders	14–38	1–11
W New York Giants	27–24	2–11
L @ Miami Dolphins	13–37	2–12
L @ Pittsburgh Steelers	10–17	2–13
W New England Patriots	29–7	3–13

Season Leaders

CATEGORY	TOTAL	PLAYER
Passing Yards	2,883	Boomer Esiason
Rushing Yards	731	Harold Green
Receiving Yards	827	Eddie Brown
Receptions	59	Eddie Brown
Interceptions	4	David Fulcher
Sacks	4	Tim Krumrie
Points	96	Jim Breech

Key Additions:
Alfred Williams (draft)

Starting Lineup

OFFENSE	POSITION
Boomer Esiason	QB
Harold Green	RB
James Brooks	RB
Eddie Brown	WR
Tim McGee	WR
Rodney Holman	TE
Anthony Munoz	LT
Bruce Reimers	LG
Bruce Kozerski	C
Ken Moyer	RG
Joe Walter	RT

DEFENSE	POSITION
Alonzo Mitz	DE
Tim Krumrie	DT
David Grant	DE
James Francis	OLB
Leo Barker	MLB
Carl Zander	MLB
Alfred Williams	OLB
Wayne Haddix	CB
Eric Thomas	CB
David Fulcher	SS
Rickey Dixon	FS

SPECIAL TEAMS	POSITION
Jim Breech	K
Eric Ball/Shane Garrett	KR
Lee Johnson	P
Mitchell Price	PR

"Leave as little
to chance as possible.
Preparation is the
key to success."

—Paul Brown

*David Fulcher was a versatile safety
who started 98 games for Cincinnati.*

1992

5–11
Fourth in AFC Central

The Bengals celebrated their 25th anniversary as a franchise in 1992, welcoming new head coach Dave Shula in the process. Cincinnati got off to a 2–0 start under Shula, but that was about all that went right in his first year.

In Week 3, Cincinnati entered the fourth quarter with a 17–3 lead over Green Bay, but a young backup quarterback named Brett Favre threw two touchdown passes to help the Packers shock the Bengals, 24–23. That loss sent the team into a tailspin. The Bengals dropped five straight games, including blowout losses to the Minnesota Vikings and Pittsburgh Steelers. Then, after back-to-back wins, they went on another five-game losing streak.

Shula opted to bench Boomer Esiason after the team fell to 4–7 following a Week 12 loss to the Detroit Lions. Esiason had completed just 51.8% of his passes for 1,407 yards, 11 touchdowns, and 15 interceptions. The Bengals turned to rookie quarterback David Klingler, whom they had taken with the sixth overall pick in the 1992 NFL Draft. Klingler struggled in his debut, completing 16 of 34 passes for 140 yards in a 21–9 loss to the Steelers.

There were some bright spots for the Bengals, despite their 5–11 record. Wide receiver Carl Pickens was named Offensive Rookie of the Year after catching 26 passes for 326 yards and one touchdown. He also returned 18 punts for 229 yards, including a 95-yard touchdown, the longest punt return in team history. Running back Harold Green made the Pro Bowl after running for 1,170 yards and two touchdowns.

NFL legend Anthony Munoz, considered by many to be the best offensive lineman of all-time, retired after the season. He dealt with knee and shoulder injuries throughout the year, which included two stints on injured reserve. He spent 12 seasons in Cincinnati, and he was a nine-time All-Pro and an 11-time Pro Bowl player. Munoz was inducted into the Pro Football Hall of Fame in 1998.

Pro Bowl Selections

- Harold Green (RB)

Schedule

	OPPONENT	SCORE	RECORD
W	@ Seattle Seahawks	21–3	1–0
W	Los Angeles Raiders (OT)	24–21	2–0
L	@ Green Bay Packers	23–24	2–1
L	Minnesota Vikings	7–42	2–2
L	Houston Oilers	24–38	2–3
L	@ Pittsburgh Steelers	0–20	2–4
L	@ Houston Oilers	10–26	2–5
W	Cleveland Browns	30–10	3–5
W	@ Chicago Bears (OT)	31–28	4–5
L	@ New York Jets	14–17	4–6
L	Detroit Lions	13–19	4–7
L	Pittsburgh Steelers	9–21	4–8
L	@ Cleveland Browns	21–37	4–9
L	@ San Diego Chargers	10–27	4–10
W	New England Patriots	20–10	5–10
L	Indianapolis Colts	17–21	5–11

Season Leaders

CATEGORY	TOTAL	PLAYER
Passing Yards	1,407	Boomer Esiason
Rushing Yards	1,170	Harold Green
Receiving Yards	408	Tim McGee
Receptions	41	Harold Green
Interceptions	4	Darryl Williams
Sacks	10	Alfred Williams
Points	88	Jim Breech

Key Additions:
David Klingler (draft), Carl Pickens (draft), Darryl Williams (draft)

Boomer Esiason was named to four Pro Bowls in his NFL career.

Starting Lineup

OFFENSE	POSITION
Boomer Esiason	QB
Harold Green	RB
Eric Ball	RB
Carl Pickens	WR
Tim McGee	WR
Rodney Holman	TE
Kevin Sargent	LT
Bruce Kozerski	LG
Mike Arthur	C
Jon Melander	RG
Joe Walter	RT

DEFENSE	POSITION
Lamar Rogers	DE
Tim Krumrie	DT
Alonzo Mitz	DE
James Francis	OLB
Ricardo McDonald	MLB
Gary Reasons	MLB
Danny Stubbs	OLB
Rod Jones	CB
Eric Thomas	CB
David Fulcher	SS
Darryl Williams	FS

SPECIAL TEAMS	POSITION
Jim Breech	K
Milt Stegall	KR
Lee Johnson	P
Carl Pickens	PR

3–13
Fourth in AFC Central

The Bengals traded quarterback Boomer Esiason to the New York Jets after the 1992 campaign for a third-round draft pick. At 32 years old, Esiason was unhappy with the direction of the franchise. The move cleared the way for second-year quarterback David Klingler.

Cincinnati continued to get younger prior to the season by releasing long-time kicker Jim Breech in favor of seventh-round draft pick Doug Pelfrey. Breech spent 13 seasons in Cincinnati and is the Bengals' all-time leader in points with 1,151. He was always clutch in the postseason, making nine of 11 field goal attempts and a perfect 25 for 25 on extra points. Breech drilled a 40-yard field goal in the fourth quarter of Super Bowl XXIII that gave the Bengals the lead.

It didn't matter who kicked for the Bengals in 1993. Klingler's run-and-shoot offense had done well in college, but the experiment didn't work in the NFL. The second-year signal-caller was a big part of Cincinnati's 0–10 start. He missed two contests with a back injury, but the Bengals were one of the worst teams in the NFL, and their record showed it.

They beat the Los Angeles Raiders, 16–10, in Week 13 for their first win. Klingler also led the Bengals to two wins in their final three games.

The offense topped the 20-point mark just once (scoring 21 points) and was held to eight or fewer points in five games. Needless to say, Cincinnati's offense finished last in scoring, averaging just 11.7 points per game. The defense fared better, though, holding opponents to 179 passing yards per game, which was second best in the NFL.

Head coach Dave Shula posted an 8–24 record in his first two seasons. Klingler was 4–13 as a starter. Serious questions arose about the future of both men following an underwhelming 1993 campaign.

Pro Bowl Selections

• None

Schedule

	OPPONENT	SCORE	RECORD
L	@ Cleveland Browns	14–27	0–1
L	Indianapolis Colts	6–9	0–2
L	@ Pittsburgh Steelers	7–34	0–3
L	Seattle Seahawks	10–19	0–4
L	@ Kansas City Chiefs	15–17	0–5
L	Cleveland Browns	17–28	0–6
L	@ Houston Oilers	12–28	0–7
L	Pittsburgh Steelers	16–24	0–8
L	Houston Oilers	3–38	0–9
L	@ New York Jets	12–17	0–10
W	Los Angeles Raiders	16–10	1–10
L	@ San Francisco 49ers	8–21	1–11
L	@ New England Patriots	2–7	1–12
W	Los Angeles Rams	15–3	2–12
W	Atlanta Falcons	21–17	3–12
L	@ New Orleans Saints	13–20	3–13

Season Leaders

CATEGORY	TOTAL	PLAYER
Passing Yards	1,935	David Klingler
Rushing Yards	589	Harold Green
Receiving Yards	654	Jeff Query
Receptions	56	Jeff Query
Interceptions	3	Michael Brim
Sacks	5	Danny Stubbs
Points	85	Doug Pelfrey

Key Additions:
John Copeland (draft), Doug Pelfrey (draft), Steve Tovar (draft)

Joe Walter was a 10-year starter on the Bengals offensive line.

Starting Lineup

OFFENSE	POSITION
David Klingler	QB
Harold Green	RB
Derrick Fenner	RB
Carl Pickens	WR
Jeff Query	WR
Tony McGee	TE
Tom Scott	LT
Ken Moyer	LG
Bruce Kozerski	C
Thomas Rayam	RG
Joe Walter	RT

DEFENSE	POSITION
John Copeland	DE
Tim Krumrie	DT
George Hinkle	DE
James Francis	OLB
Eric Shaw	MLB
Ricardo McDonald	MLB
Alfred Williams	OLB
Michael Brim	CB
Rod Jones	CB
Lance Gunn	SS
Darryl Williams	FS

SPECIAL TEAMS	POSITION
Doug Pelfrey	K
Patrick Robinson	KR
Lee Johnson	P
Patrick Robinson	PR

1994

3–13
Third in AFC Central

Bengals owner Mike Brown stuck with head coach Dave Shula and quarterback David Klingler in 1994, despite their struggles on the field.

Cincinnati took defensive tackle Dan "Big Daddy" Wilkinson with the top pick in the 1994 NFL Draft. They hoped he would be a perfect fit for their switch to a 4–3 defense. Wilkinson went on to start 14 games as a rookie, finishing with 44 tackles and 5.5 sacks.

Klingler started the first seven games, and nothing changed. The team started the season 0–7. The former sixth-overall pick threw six touchdowns, nine interceptions, and posted a 65.3 quarterback rating over that span. Klingler and backup quarterback Donald Hollas both suffered injuries in Cincinnati's Week 7 loss to Cleveland. The injuries paved the way for Jeff Blake, who had joined the Bengals after being released by the New York Jets in August. Cincinnati lost to the Dallas Cowboys in Blake's first start, but he helped them build a 14–0 lead, which included two long touchdown passes to rookie wide receiver Darnay Scott.

Blake's performance improved the following week, as he led the Bengals to a 20–17 win over the Seahawks in Seattle, completing 31 of 43 passes for 387 yards. The following week he led Cincinnati to a 34–31 win over Houston. He threw for 354 yards and four touchdowns. Cincinnati's offense had come alive with the 24-year-old at quarterback.

Blake quickly became a local cult hero. He was dubbed "Shake-N-Blake," and his nickname was even printed on T-shirts. Fans finally had a reason to be hopeful. Unfortunately, the excitement died down as the Bengals lost their next five games.

Cincinnati beat the Philadelphia Eagles in the season finale when Doug Pelfrey kicked two field goals in the final three seconds in the 33–30 win. He made a 22-yarder to tie the game and then booted a 54-yarder after the Eagles muffed the short kickoff.

Longtime defensive tackle Tim Krumrie retired after the 1994 campaign. He appeared in 188 regular-season games over his 12-year career. He was a two-time Pro Bowl player and a one-time All-Pro.

Schedule

OPPONENT	SCORE	RECORD
L Cleveland Browns	20–28	0–1
L @ San Diego Chargers	10–27	0–2
L New England Patriots	28–31	0–3
L @ Houston Oilers	13–20	0–4
L Miami Dolphins	7–23	0–5
L @ Pittsburgh Steelers	10–14	0–6
L @ Cleveland Browns	13–37	0–7
L Dallas Cowboys	20–23	0–8
W @ Seattle Seahawks (OT)	20–17	1–8
W Houston Oilers	34–31	2–8
L Indianapolis Colts	13–17	2–9
L @ Denver Broncos	13–15	2–10
L Pittsburgh Steelers	15–38	2–11
L @ New York Giants	20–27	2–12
L @ Arizona Cardinals	7–28	2–13
W Philadelphia Eagles	33–30	3–13

Season Leaders

CATEGORY	TOTAL	PLAYER
Passing Yards	2,154	Jeff Blake
Rushing Yards	468	Derrick Fenner
Receiving Yards	1,127	Carl Pickens
Receptions	71	Carl Pickens
Interceptions	3	Louis Oliver
Sacks	5	Danny Stubbs
Points	108	Doug Pelfrey

Key Additions:
Jeff Blake (free agent), Rich Braham (waivers), Darrick Brilz (free agent), Darnay Scott (draft), Dan Wilkinson (draft)

Starting Lineup

Harold Green — RB

Jeff Blake — QB

Derrick Fenner — RB

Carl Pickens — WR
CB Rod Jones

Kevin Sargent — LT
DE Alfred Williams

Dave Cadigan — LG
DT Dan Wilkinson

Darrick Brilz — C

Ken Moyer — RG
DT Keith Rucker

Bruce Kozerski — RT
DE John Copeland

Tony McGee — TE

Darnay Scott — WR
CB Michael Brim

LB Ricardo McDonald

LB Steve Tovar

LB James Francis

SS Louis Oliver

FS Darryl Williams

K   Doug Pelfrey
KR Eric Ball
P   Lee Johnson
PR Corey Sawyer

Bengals Trivia

As a nose tackle in 1988, Tim Krumrie had an eye-popping 152 total tackles.

Shake-N-Blake

1994

Pro Bowl Selections

• None

1995

7–9
Third in AFC Central

The Bengals were hoping to take a major step forward in 1995 when they traded up in the draft to take Penn State running back Ki-Jana Carter with the top pick. The trade up for Carter was the first time Cincinnati had ever moved up in the first round of the NFL draft.

However, Carter never took a regular-season snap as a rookie. He missed the first two preseason games with an ankle sprain and then suffered a season-ending knee injury on his third carry in a preseason matchup against the Detroit Lions.

With the top pick out of commission, the Bengals offense leaned on the arm of Jeff Blake, and he rose to the occasion. Blake threw for 3,822 yards and 28 touchdowns. He also ran for 309 yards and two more scores.

Blake's chemistry with wide receiver Carl Pickens was second to none. Pickens set a team record and led the NFL with 17 touchdown catches. (The mark still stands as the most touchdowns by a Bengal in a season.)

Cincinnati won their first two games but dropped four of their next five. After falling to 3–6, the Bengals won a game, then lost the next—and continued that pattern for the remainder of the season.

The team provided some fun moments and were much better than they had been in previous seasons under head coach Dave Shula. But they still finished 7–9 and were eliminated from playoff contention in Week 15.

Pickens finished with 99 receptions for 1,234 yards. Darnay Scott came in second on the team in receiving, finishing with 821 yards. Tight end Tony McGee had his best season in the pros, posting a career-high 55 catches for 754 yards.

Pro Bowl Selections

- Jeff Blake (QB)
- Carl Pickens (WR)

Schedule

OPPONENT	SCORE	RECORD
W @ Indianapolis Colts (OT)	24–21	1–0
W Jacksonville Jaguars	24–17	2–0
L @ Seattle Seahawks	21–24	2–1
L Houston Oilers	28–38	2–2
L Miami Dolphins	23–26	2–3
L @ Tampa Bay Buccaneers	16–19	2–4
W @ Pittsburgh Steelers	27–9	3–4
L Cleveland Browns (OT)	26–29	3–5
L Oakland Raiders	17–20	3–6
W @ Houston Oilers	32–25	4–6
L Pittsburgh Steelers	31–49	4–7
W @ Jacksonville Jaguars	17–13	5–7
L @ Green Bay Packers	10–24	5–8
W Chicago Bears	16–10	6–8
L @ Cleveland Browns	10–26	6–9
W Minnesota Vikings	27–24	7–9

Season Leaders

CATEGORY	TOTAL	PLAYER
Passing Yards	3,822	Jeff Blake
Rushing Yards	661	Harold Green
Receiving Yards	1,234	Carl Pickens
Receptions	99	Carl Pickens
Interceptions	4	Bracy Walker
Sacks	9	John Copeland
Points	121	Doug Pelfrey

Key Additions:
Ki-Jana Carter (draft)

Kicker Doug Pelfrey and head coach Dave Shula celebrate a walk-off win.

Starting Lineup

OFFENSE	POSITION
Jeff Blake	QB
Harold Green	RB
Jeff Cothran	RB
Carl Pickens	WR
Darnay Scott	WR
Tony McGee	TE
Kevin Sargent	LT
Scott Brumfield	LG
Darrick Brilz	C
Todd Kalis	RG
Joe Walter	RT

DEFENSE	POSITION
John Copeland	DE
Dan Wilkinson	DT
Keith Rucker	DT
Artie Smith	DE
James Francis	OLB
Steve Tovar	MLB
Ricardo McDonald	OLB
Roger Jones	CB
Rod Jones	CB
Bracy Walker	SS
Darryl Williams	FS

SPECIAL TEAMS	POSITION
Doug Pelfrey	K
David Dunn	KR
Lee Johnson	P
Corey Sawyer	PR

8–8
Third in AFC Central

There was hope that Cincinnati could make a playoff push in 1996, but Jeff Blake and the Bengals got off to a slow start. They lost six of their first seven games. That, combined with a blown 21–0 lead in Week 8 against the San Francisco 49ers, sealed the fate of head coach Dave Shula.

Owner Mike Brown fired Shula. The coach posted a 19–52 record and became the fastest coach in NFL history to lose 50 games.

Cincinnati promoted offensive coordinator Bruce Coslet to interim head coach. The move worked, as the Bengals won three straight games. Coslet's most impressive win came against Baltimore in Week 10. Cincinnati rallied from a 21–3 halftime deficit on the road to win, 24–21.

The Bengals went 7–2 down the stretch to finish 8–8 on the season. The run included two wins over the Ravens, a win over the Pittsburgh Steelers, and a victory over the Indianapolis Colts in the season finale.

Blake proved his breakout 1995 campaign wasn't a fluke, throwing for 3,624 yards, 24 touchdowns, and 14 interceptions. He also ran for 317 yards and two scores.

Carl Pickens led the AFC with 100 receptions, which also set a Bengals' single-season record. He finished with 1,180 yards and 12 touchdowns. Pickens made his second straight Pro Bowl.

Ashley Ambrose finished with eight interceptions at the cornerback spot and also made the Pro Bowl.

The Bengals signed Coslet to a four-year contract extension before the end of the season. His team won their final three games, and the arrow was pointing upward going into the 1997 season.

Pro Bowl Selections

- Ashley Ambrose (CB)
- Carl Pickens (WR)

Schedule

	OPPONENT	SCORE	RECORD
L	@ Saint Louis Rams	16–26	0–1
L	@ San Diego Chargers	14–27	0–2
W	New Orleans Saints	30–15	1–2
L	Denver Broncos	10–14	1–3
L	Houston Oilers (OT)	27–30	1–4
L	@ Pittsburgh Steelers	10–20	1–5
L	@ San Francisco 49ers	21–28	1–6
W	Jacksonville Jaguars	28–21	2–6
W	@ Baltimore Ravens	24–21	3–6
W	Pittsburgh Steelers	34–24	4–6
L	@ Buffalo Bills	17–31	4–7
W	Atlanta Falcons	41–31	5–7
L	@ Jacksonville Jaguars	27–30	5–8
W	Baltimore Ravens	21–14	6–8
W	@ Houston Oilers	21–13	7–8
W	Indianapolis Colts	31–24	8–8

Season Leaders

CATEGORY	TOTAL	PLAYER
Passing Yards	3,624	Jeff Blake
Rushing Yards	847	Garrison Hearst
Receiving Yards	1,180	Carl Pickens
Receptions	100	Carl Pickens
Interceptions	8	Ashley Ambrose
Sacks	6.5	Dan Wilkinson
Points	110	Doug Pelfrey

Key Additions:
Ashley Ambrose (free agent), Willie Anderson (draft), Garrison Hearst (free agent)

Carl Pickens had four 1,000-yard receiving seasons with Cincinnati.

Starting Lineup

OFFENSE	POSITION
Jeff Blake	QB
Garrison Hearst	RB
Jeff Cothran	RB
Carl Pickens	WR
Darnay Scott	WR
Tony McGee	TE
Willie Anderson	LT
Rich Braham	LG
Darrick Brilz	C
Ken Blackman	RG
Joe Walter	RT

DEFENSE	POSITION
John Copeland	DE
Dan Wilkinson	DT
Tim Johnson	DT
Artie Smith	DE
James Francis	OLB
Steve Tovar	MLB
Ricardo McDonald	OLB
Ashley Ambrose	CB
Jimmy Spencer	CB
Bracy Walker	SS
Bo Orlando	FS

SPECIAL TEAMS	POSITION
Doug Pelfrey	K
David Dunn	KR
Lee Johnson	P
Corey Sawyer	PR

7–9
Fourth in AFC Central

After posting a 7–2 record down the stretch in 1996, there were plenty of reasons for optimism entering the 1997 campaign. The Bengals were hoping Bruce Coslet could lead them to the playoffs for the first time since 1990.

After spending training camp in Wilmington, Ohio, for the previous 29 seasons, the Bengals opened a new facility in Georgetown, Kentucky. The team also re-signed quarterback Boomer Esiason to a one-year contract. He returned to serve as Jeff Blake's backup nearly a decade after leading Cincinnati to Super Bowl XXIII.

The Bengals beat the Arizona Cardinals in their season opener but lost the next seven games. Despite having an offensive mind like Coslet as head coach and having Blake under center, the team struggled to score. Cincinnati averaged just 15.5 points in their first eight games and topped the 20-point mark just three times.

Esiason showed that he could still play at a high level in Week 11 when Blake suffered a concussion. Esiason completed seven of 10 passes for 82 yards and two touchdowns in a 28–13 win.

Blake returned for the Week 12 matchup against Pittsburgh. The Steelers dismantled their division rival, 20–3, and the Bengals turned to Esiason for their final five games. The former MVP posted a 4–1 record in five starts. The offense topped the 30-point mark four times and averaged 32.2 points per game during that stretch.

Cincinnati finished with a 7–9 record, and Esiason left the NFL on a high note. He retired and took a broadcasting job on Monday Night Football.

Rookie running back Corey Dillon flashed potential throughout the year. He ran for 246 yards and four touchdowns in Week 15 against Tennessee, setting an NFL record for rushing yards in a game by a rookie.

Pro Bowl Selections

• None

Schedule

OPPONENT	SCORE	RECORD
W Arizona Cardinals	24–21	1–0
L @ Baltimore Ravens	10–23	1–1
L @ Denver Broncos	20–38	1–2
L New York Jets	14–31	1–3
L @ Jacksonville Jaguars	13–21	1–4
L @ Tennessee Oilers	7–30	1–5
L Pittsburgh Steelers	10–26	1–6
L @ New York Giants	27–29	1–7
W San Diego Chargers	38–31	2–7
W @ Indianapolis Colts	28–13	3–7
L @ Pittsburgh Steelers	3–20	3–8
W Jacksonville Jaguars	31–26	4–8
L @ Philadelphia Eagles	42–44	4–9
W Tennessee Oilers	41–14	5–9
W Dallas Cowboys	31–24	6–9
W Baltimore Ravens	16–14	7–9

Season Leaders

CATEGORY	TOTAL	PLAYER
Passing Yards	2,125	Jeff Blake
Rushing Yards	1,129	Corey Dillon
Receiving Yards	797	Darnay Scott
Receptions	54	Darnay Scott
Interceptions	4	Corey Sawyer
Sacks	8.5	Gerald Dixon
Points	77	Doug Pelfrey

Key Additions:
Corey Dillon (draft),
Boomer Esiason (free agent)

Starting Lineup

OFFENSE	POSITION
Jeff Blake	QB
Corey Dillon	RB
Brian Milne	RB
Carl Pickens	WR
Darnay Scott	WR
Tony McGee	TE
Kevin Sargent	LT
Rich Braham	LG
Darrick Brilz	C
Ken Blackman	RG
Willie Anderson	RT

DEFENSE	POSITION
John Copeland	DE
Kimo von Oelhoffen	DT
Dan Wilkinson	DE
James Francis	OLB
Tom Tumulty	MLB
Ricardo McDonald	MLB
Gerald Dixon	OLB
Ashley Ambrose	CB
Jimmy Spencer	CB
Sam Shade	SS
Greg Myers	FS

SPECIAL TEAMS	POSITION
Doug Pelfrey	K
Eric Bieniemy	KR
Lee Johnson	P
Greg Myers	PR

In 11 seasons with the Bengals, Lee Johnson averaged 43.2 yards per punt.

"Everyone is
needed,
but no one is
necessary."
—Bruce Coslet

Hall-of-Famers

To date, Anthony Munoz and Ken Riley are the only two Bengals players inducted into the Pro Football Hall of Fame.

Munoz is widely considered the greatest offensive lineman of all-time. He made 11 straight Pro Bowls from 1981 to 1991 and was a nine-time All-Pro at left tackle. Munoz was a big reason why Cincinnati won two AFC championships in the 1980s (1981, 1988). He protected Ken Anderson and Boomer Esiason during their MVP seasons, and he cleared the way for running backs like Pete Johnson, James Brooks, Ickey Woods, Harold Green, and Larry Kinnebrew. Munoz played in 185 career games, which is seventh most in Bengals history. He was inducted into the Pro Football Hall of Fame in 1998.

Riley, like Munoz, played at an elite level for more than a decade. After switching from quarterback to cornerback in 1969, he quickly established himself as a mainstay on Paul Brown's defense and lasted through the 1983 season. He finished his career with 65 interceptions, including eight takeaways in his final year. Riley had five career pick-sixes and appeared in 207 games, the second most in team history. He helped Cincinnati reach Super Bowl XVI, and he helped Coach Brown lay a foundation of success for the new franchise. Riley was inducted into the Pro Football Hall of Fame in 2023.

Brown was inducted into the Pro Football Hall of Fame in 1967, as a member of the Cleveland Browns. Wide receivers Charlie Joiner and Terrell Owens are also hall-of-famers, but they spent most of their careers on other teams. Joiner played for the Bengals from 1972 to 1975, and Owens was in Cincinnati for the 2010 campaign.

Anthony Munoz (78) was Cincinnati's first inductee into the Pro Football Hall of Fame.

1998

3–13
Fifth in AFC Central

With Jeff Blake's struggles and with Boomer Esiason's retirement, the Bengals opted to move in another direction at quarterback ahead of the 1998 season. They signed veteran Neil O'Donnell to a four-year, $17 million contract.

Cincinnati hoped the veteran would end their decade-long search for a franchise quarterback. Instead, O'Donnell became the latest signal-caller to struggle on the banks of the Ohio.

The 32-year-old beat out Blake for the starting job in training camp, but that's where the winning stopped. O'Donnell posted a 2–9 record as a starter, completing 61.8% of his passes for 2,216 yards, with 15 touchdowns and four interceptions.

Blake started two games late in the season before missing the final three contests due to an injury. Cincinnati turned to reserve quarterbacks Paul Justin and Eric Kresser down the stretch. The Bengals finished with a 3–13 record, their worst mark since 1994.

Corey Dillon ran for 1,130 yards and four touchdowns, becoming the only Bengals running back to rush for 1,000 or more yards in each of his first two seasons. Carl Pickens led the team in receiving, finishing with 82 receptions for 1,023 yards and five touchdowns.

The shine from head coach Bruce Coslet's successful stint in 1996 had worn off, and there were serious questions about the direction of the franchise following the 1998 campaign. The Bengals had talented players like Dillon and Pickens, but patience was wearing thin. The team didn't have a long-term answer at quarterback.

At 3–13, Cincinnati secured the third pick in the 1999 NFL Draft behind the expansion Cleveland Browns (whose original team had moved to Baltimore in 1996) and the Philadelphia Eagles.

Schedule

OPPONENT	SCORE	RECORD
L Tennessee Oilers	14–23	0–1
W @ Detroit Lions (OT)	34–28	1–1
L Green Bay Packers	6–13	1–2
L @ Baltimore Ravens	24–31	1–3
W Pittsburgh Steelers	25–20	2–3
L @ Tennessee Oilers	14–44	2–4
L @ Oakland Raiders	10–27	2–5
L Denver Broncos	26–33	2–6
L @ Jacksonville Jaguars	11–24	2–7
L @ Minnesota Vikings	3–24	2–8
L Baltimore Ravens	13–20	2–9
L Jacksonville Jaguars	17–34	2–10
L Buffalo Bills	20–33	2–11
L @ Indianapolis Colts	26–39	2–12
W @ Pittsburgh Steelers	25–34	3–12
L Tampa Bay Buccaneers	0–35	3–13

Season Leaders

CATEGORY	TOTAL	PLAYER
Passing Yards	2,216	Neil O'Donnell
Rushing Yards	1,130	Corey Dillon
Receiving Yards	1,023	Carl Pickens
Receptions	82	Carl Pickens
Interceptions	3	A. Hawkins, S. Shade
Sacks	6	Reinard Wilson
Points	78	Doug Pelfrey

Key Additions:
Neil O'Donnell (free agent), Brian Simmons (draft), Takeo Spikes (draft)

Starting Lineup

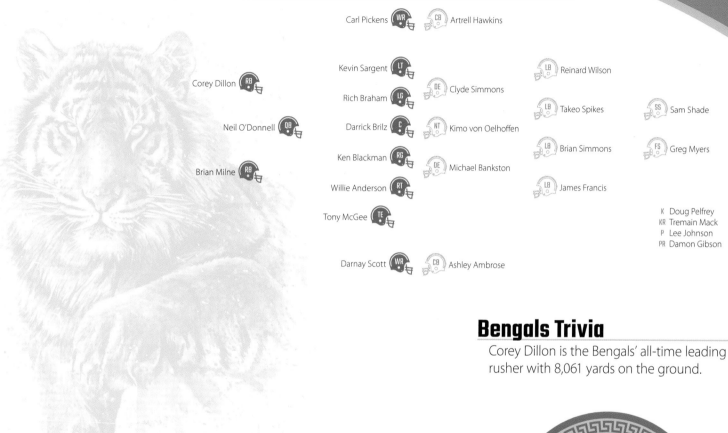

Carl Pickens (WR)   (CB) Artrell Hawkins

Corey Dillon (RB)

Kevin Sargent (LT)   (LB) Reinard Wilson

Neil O'Donnell (QB)

Rich Braham (LG)   (DE) Clyde Simmons

Darrick Brilz (C)   (NT) Kimo von Oelhoffen   (LB) Takeo Spikes   (SS) Sam Shade

Brian Milne (RB)

Ken Blackman (RG)   (DE) Michael Bankston   (LB) Brian Simmons   (FS) Greg Myers

Willie Anderson (RT)   (LB) James Francis

Tony McGee (TE)

K Doug Pelfrey
KR Tremain Mack
P Lee Johnson
PR Damon Gibson

Darnay Scott (WR)   (CB) Ashley Ambrose

Bengals Trivia

Corey Dillon is the Bengals' all-time leading rusher with 8,061 yards on the ground.

Pro Bowl Selections

• None

Dillon surpasses
1,000 yards again

1998

4–12

Fifth in AFC Central

The 1990s hadn't been kind to the Bengals, but they were hoping to end the decade on a high note when they took quarterback Akili Smith with the third overall pick in the 1999 NFL Draft. The Bengals loved Smith so much that they turned down a trade offer from the New Orleans Saints that included three first-round picks, two second-round picks, and the rest of New Orleans' picks in the 1999 draft. Owner Mike Brown believed Smith could change the franchise. Instead, he fit right in with their losing culture.

After holding out for most of training camp, Smith eventually signed a seven-year, $56 million contract. Missing camp didn't help his chances of succeeding as a rookie. Smith didn't start in the season-opening loss to the Tennessee Titans and didn't play versus the Carolina Panthers. He struggled in outings against the San Diego Chargers and Saint Louis Rams.

The Bengals started 0–4 for the first time since 1994, but Smith did give fans some hope in Week 5, leading Cincinnati past Cleveland in the Battle of Ohio. He went up against fellow rookie quarterback Tim Couch, who had been the top pick in the 1999 NFL Draft. Smith played what would be the best game of his career, completing 25 of 42 passes for 221 yards and two touchdowns.

The Bengals trailed 17–12 late in the fourth quarter when Smith took the Bengals on an 80-yard touchdown drive. He threw a perfect ball to Carl Pickens for a two-yard touchdown in the corner of the end zone with five seconds to go, lifting Cincinnati to an 18–17 win.

Smith was only active for three more games in 1999 and completed just 52% of his passes. His touchdown toss to Pickens was the last one he threw all season. Jeff Blake and Scott Covington took over quarterback duties, but Cincinnati's season was already over.

Pro Bowl Selections

- Corey Dillon (RB)
- Tremain Mack (KR)

Schedule

OPPONENT	SCORE	RECORD
L @ Tennessee Titans	35–36	0–1
L San Diego Chargers (OT)	7–34	0–2
L @ Carolina Panthers	3–27	0–3
L Saint Louis Rams	10–38	0–4
W @ Cleveland Browns	18–17	1–4
L Pittsburgh Steelers	3–17	1–5
L @ Indianapolis Colts	10–31	1–6
L Jacksonville Jaguars	10–41	1–7
L @ Seattle Seahawks	20–37	1–8
L Tennessee Titans	14–24	1–9
L Baltimore Ravens	31–34	1–10
W @ Pittsburgh Steelers	27–20	2–10
W San Francisco 49ers	44–30	3–10
W Cleveland Browns	44–28	4–10
L @ Baltimore Ravens	0–22	4–11
L @ Jacksonville Jaguars	7–24	4–12

Season Leaders

CATEGORY	TOTAL	PLAYER
Passing Yards	2,670	Jeff Blake
Rushing Yards	1,200	Corey Dillon
Receiving Yards	1,022	Darnay Scott
Receptions	68	Darnay Scott
Interceptions	3	Rodney Heath
Sacks	6	Michael Bankston
Points	81	Doug Pelfrey

Key Additions:
Akili Smith (draft)

Brian Simmons had 114 tackles and five passes defended in 1999.

Starting Lineup

OFFENSE	POSITION
Jeff Blake	QB
Corey Dillon	RB
Clif Groce	RB
Carl Pickens	WR
Darnay Scott	WR
Tony McGee	TE
Rod Jones	LT
Matt O'Dwyer	LG
Rich Braham	C
Jay Leeuwenburg	RG
Willie Anderson	RT

DEFENSE	POSITION
John Copeland	DE
Oliver Gibson	DT
Michael Bankston	DE
Steve Foley	OLB
Brian Simmons	MLB
Takeo Spikes	MLB
Adrian Ross	OLB
Rodney Heath	CB
Artrell Hawkins	CB
Myron Bell	SS
Cory Hall	FS

SPECIAL TEAMS	POSITION
Doug Pelfrey	K
Tremain Mack	KR
Will Brice	P
Damon Griffin	PR

All-1990s Offense

QUARTERBACK: The Bengals struggled for most of the 1990s, but their offense did have some bright spots. **Jeff Blake** (1994–1999) knocked Boomer Esiason out of his second all-decade team. Blake completed 55.8% of his passes for 15,134 yards and 93 touchdowns in 75 career games. Blake was a Pro Bowl player in 1995 and led the NFL with five game-winning drives in 1996.

RUNNING BACKS: **Corey Dillon** (1997–1999) led the way at running back at the end of the decade. He averaged 4.6 yards per attempt, had 21 total touchdowns, and set the NFL rookie record for rushing yards in a game (246). Dillon leads the Bengals in all-time rushing yards (8,061) and is third in rushing touchdowns (45). **Harold Green** (1990–1995) is an obvious choice for the other spot. He ran for 3,727 yards and eight touchdowns in 86 career games. He also had 145 receptions for 1,004 yards and three scores.

WIDE RECEIVERS: **Carl Pickens** (1992–1999) is a runaway choice at wide receiver. He was named Offensive Rookie of the Year in 1992 and made two Pro Bowls in eight seasons. Pickens is fourth in team history in receiving yards (6,887), third in receiving touchdowns (63), and third in receptions (530). **Darnay Scott** (1994–1999) is one of the most underrated Bengals of all time. He usually played second fiddle to Pickens, but he posted 329 receptions for 5,156 yards and 34 touchdowns in 93 games. He averaged 15.7 yards per catch during that span.

TIGHT END: Tony McGee (1993–1999) made 111 starts and only missed one game between 1993 and 1999. He had 259 receptions for 3,338 yards and 18 touchdowns over that span.

TACKLES: **Anthony Munoz** (1990–1992) makes a second all-decade team. He was a Pro Bowl selection in two of his three seasons and was a first-team All-Pro in 1990, which was the only season of the decade that saw Cincinnati make the playoffs. **Joe Walter** (1990–1997) was a standout on the right side of the line. He started 93 contests and appeared in 99 games.

GUARDS: The interior offensive line experienced a lot of shuffling throughout the decade. **Rich Braham** (1994–1999) spent significant time at both center and guard during his career, but he played left guard from 1996 to 1998, starting 44 games and solidifying that spot in the trenches. **Ken Moyer** (1990–1994) appeared in 63 games, making 54 starts.

CENTER: **Bruce Kozerski** (1990–1995) made 87 starts. He showed off his versatility by spending time at guard and tackle. However, he stood out at the center position.

KICKER: **Doug Pelfrey** (1993–1999) had big shoes to fill following Jim Breech, but he delivered, appearing in 111 games. Pelfrey made 77.3% of his field goal attempts, including eight field goals of 50 yards or more. He converted 97.1% of his extra-point attempts.

KICK RETURNER: **Tremain Mack** (1996–1999) is the Bengals' all-time leader in kickoff-return yardage with 3,583 yards. He returned 96 kicks for 2,547 yards—an average of 26.5 yards per return—and two touchdowns in the decade.

Statistics for the all-decade team are for the given decade only, unless otherwise noted.

All-1990s Defense

DEFENSIVE ENDS: John Copeland (1993–1999) appeared in 91 games, making 86 starts and racking up 285 tackles, 23 sacks, and three interceptions. He recovered two fumbles, one of them for a touchdown. **Alfred Williams** (1991–1994) had 157 tackles and 26.5 sacks in four seasons after being taken in the first round of the 1991 NFL Draft.

DEFENSIVE TACKLES: Tim Krumrie (1990–1994) did enough in the 1990s to make the team in back-to-back decades. Krumrie started 67 games and finished with 358 tackles. He also had 14 sacks and three forced fumbles. **Dan "Big Daddy" Wilkinson** (1994–1997) might not have fully lived up to expectations after being the top pick in the 1994 NFL Draft, but he was productive for four seasons, finishing with 162 tackles, 25 sacks, and two forced fumbles in 61 games. He joins Krumrie in the defensive tackle room.

LINEBACKERS: James Francis (1990–1998) leads the pack at linebacker with 129 career starts, 556 tackles, 33 sacks, and 11 interceptions in nine seasons. He returned three of those interceptions for touchdowns. **Ricardo McDonald** (1992–1997) had 430 tackles and 13 sacks in six seasons. He also forced four fumbles and recovered two fumbles. **Steve Tovar** (1993–1997) edges out Takeo Spikes for the final spot. Tovar had 436 tackles, seven interceptions, and five forced fumbles in 73 career games.

CORNERBACKS: Rod Jones (1990–1996) signed with Cincinnati as a free agent. He went on to play in 87 games (62 starts), finishing with 292 tackles, six interceptions, and four fumble recoveries. **Ashley Ambrose** (1996–1998) only spent three seasons in Cincinnati, but in 1996 he led the team with eight interceptions, made the Pro Bowl,

and was a first-team All-Pro. He had 149 tackles and 13 interceptions, returning one for a touchdown, during his time with the team.

SAFETIES: David Fulcher (1990–1992) also makes the team for the second decade in a row. He was a Pro Bowl player and a second-team All-Pro in 1990 when he had four interceptions, a safety, and 53 solo tackles. He intercepted 11 passes in three years. **Darryl Williams** (1992–1995) made 60 starts and tallied 401 tackles, nine interceptions, and six sacks. He scored a touchdown and also a safety.

PUNTER: Lee Johnson (1990–1998) averaged 43.5 yards per punt and appeared in 141 games.

PUNT RETURNER: Mitchell Price (1990–1993) is the punt returner of the decade after averaging 10.6 yards per return in two full seasons with the Bengals. He scored a touchdown in 1990 and another during the 1991 season. Price also spent parts of the 1992 and 1993 seasons with the Bengals.

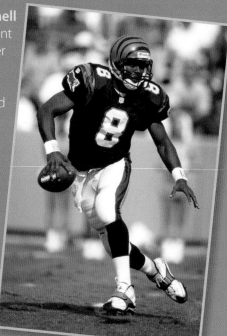

Jeff Blake rushed for 1,499 yards from the quarterback position.

4–12
Fifth in AFC Central

After sharing Riverfront Stadium with the Cincinnati Reds for more than three decades, the Bengals finally got a home of their own when Paul Brown Stadium officially opened on August 19, 2000. Cincinnati beat the Chicago Bears in Week 4 of the preseason—the first event ever held at the new stadium.

Unfortunately for the home team, they struggled when the regular season began. Cincinnati started 0–3 and were outscored 74–7 in those games (their lowest point total in a three-game stretch since 1978). To make matters worse, they lost their head coach in the process. Bruce Coslet unexpectedly quit on September 25, 2000. Coslet was 21–39 in five seasons as head coach. Owner Mike Brown named defensive coordinator Dick LeBeau as the interim head coach.

The team showed signs of improvement after the shakeup but didn't win a game until Week 8, when Corey Dillon put together a historic performance. The star running back ran for an NFL-record 278 yards and two touchdowns, guiding the Bengals to a 31–21 win versus Denver. (See page 92.)

The Bengals beat the Browns the following week, but there wouldn't be a run in the second half of the season. Instead, Cincinnati lost six of their final eight games to finish 4–12 for a second consecutive year.

The Bengals' struggles at quarterback continued. The franchise had hoped that Akili Smith would take a step forward in his second year, but he completed just 44.2% of his passes and posted a 2–9 record as a starter.

Smith was already being called a bust after failing to flash much potential in his first two NFL seasons. Rookie wide receiver Peter Warrick also struggled, largely due to the team's instability at quarterback. Smith was benched in favor of reserve Scott Mitchell for the final month of the season. Mitchell started five games and posted a 2–3 record.

Dillon was a shining star in what was otherwise an awful season. He ran for 1,435 yards and seven touchdowns, averaging 4.6 yards per carry.

Schedule

OPPONENT	SCORE	RECORD
L Cleveland Browns	7–24	0–1
L @ Jacksonville Jaguars	0–13	0–2
L @ Baltimore Ravens	0–37	0–3
L Miami Dolphins	16–31	0–4
L Tennessee Titans	14–23	0–5
L @ Pittsburgh Steelers	0–15	0–6
W Denver Broncos	31–21	1–6
W @ Cleveland Browns	12–3	2–6
L Baltimore Ravens	7–27	2–7
L @ Dallas Cowboys	6–23	2–8
L @ New England Patriots	13–16	2–9
L Pittsburgh Steelers	28–48	2–10
W Arizona Cardinals	24–13	3–10
L @ Tennessee Titans	3–35	3–11
W Jacksonville Jaguars	17–14	4–11
L @ Philadelphia Eagles	7–16	4–12

Season Leaders

CATEGORY	TOTAL	PLAYER
Passing Yards	1,253	Akili Smith
Rushing Yards	1,435	Corey Dillon
Receiving Yards	592	Peter Warrick
Receptions	51	Peter Warrick
Interceptions	2	T. Carter, T. Spikes
Sacks	4	S. Foley, O. Gibson, C. Hall
Points	57	Neil Rackers

Key Additions:
Peter Warrick (draft)

Starting Lineup

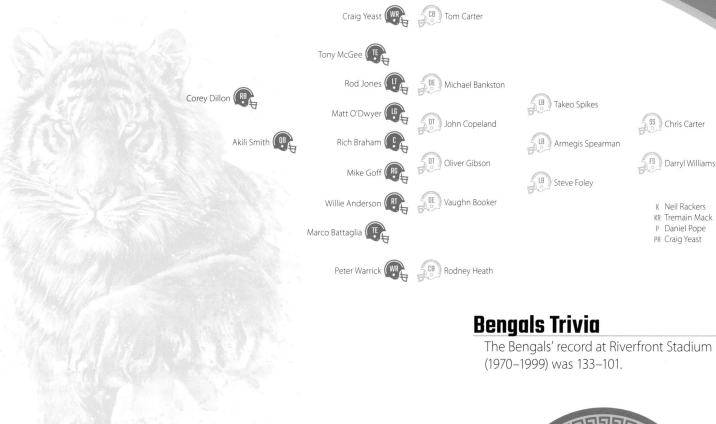

Craig Yeast (WR) — (CB) Tom Carter

Tony McGee (TE)

Rod Jones (LT) — (DE) Michael Bankston

Corey Dillon (RB)

Matt O'Dwyer (LG) — (DT) John Copeland

Akili Smith (QB)

Rich Braham (C)

Mike Goff (RG) — (DT) Oliver Gibson

Willie Anderson (RT) — (DE) Vaughn Booker

Marco Battaglia (TE)

Peter Warrick (WR) — (CB) Rodney Heath

(LB) Takeo Spikes

(LB) Armegis Spearman — (SS) Chris Carter

(LB) Steve Foley — (FS) Darryl Williams

K Neil Rackers
KR Tremain Mack
P Daniel Pope
PR Craig Yeast

Bengals Trivia

The Bengals' record at Riverfront Stadium (1970–1999) was 133–101.

Pro Bowl Selections

• Corey Dillon (RB)

Dillon sets NFL rushing record

2000

Dillon Runs Wild

The 2000 Bengals left plenty to be desired for most of the season, but running back Corey Dillon gave fans a reason to cheer in Week 8 against the Denver Broncos at Paul Brown Stadium. He rushed for an NFL record 278 yards versus the second-best rushing defense in the league, breaking the record of NFL legend Walter Payton (275 yards), which had stood for 23 seasons.

Cincinnati entered the game on October 22 with a 0–6 record, and they trailed in the second quarter, 14–3. But Dillon—and the Bengals' rushing attack—was effective throughout the game. Dillon went for 26 yards on his second carry. He followed that with a 31-yard run on the following possession.

Dillon seemed to break multiple tackles every time he touched the ball. Even after a few short gains, he responded with a 21-yard run on the Bengals' fourth possession. Denver had a 14–10 lead at the half, but the star running back was just getting warmed up.

Dillon continued to gain big chunks of yards at a time. He added a 37-yarder on Cincinnati's first drive of the second half, then a 30-yarder on their second possession of the third quarter. Dillon's 65-yard touchdown run with 5:09 remaining in the fourth quarter gave the Bengals a commanding 24–14 lead. He followed that with a 41-yard touchdown with less than two minutes remaining to clinch the 31–21 victory. It was the Bengals' first win of the season.

Dillon set the record for most rushing yards in an NFL game, finishing with 278 yards and two touchdowns on 22 carries. His offensive line and fullback Clif Groce did a wonderful job of opening up lanes. The mark has been broken multiple times since, but it remains the most rushing yards in a game in franchise history—and a memorable day for Bengals fans.

6–10
Sixth in AFC Central

No one expected much from the Bengals in 2001, but the team surprised people early in the season. Cincinnati beat New England in the opener, before taking down Baltimore in Week 2. The victory over the Ravens gave the Bengals their first 2–0 start since 1995.

The Bengals dropped their next two games, road matchups against the San Diego Chargers and Pittsburgh Steelers. Unlike in previous seasons, they responded to adversity by winning two of their next three games to enter the bye week with a 4–3 record.

However, all the momentum they appeared to build came to a screeching halt in the second half of the season. After scoring 31 points in a win over Detroit, the team didn't score more than 14 points in each of their next seven games—all losses. The Bengals went from 4–3 to 4–10 in a hurry and failed to make the playoffs for an 11th straight year.

Cincinnati closed the season with back-to-back wins, beating the Steelers in overtime and the Tennessee Titans in Nashville. A 6–10 record was a two-win improvement, but it wasn't enough to get the Bengals into legitimate playoff contention.

Running back Corey Dillon made the Pro Bowl for a third consecutive season. He ran for 1,315 yards and 10 touchdowns. He also had three touchdown receptions. Former first rounder Akili Smith continued to disappoint at quarterback, which opened the door for Jon Kitna, who earned the starting job after signing with the Bengals in free agency. Kitna started 15 games for Cincinnati, posting a 6–9 record.

The Bengals put together one of their finest drafts in franchise history. They took defensive end Justin Smith with the fourth overall pick and added multiple key pieces, including wide receivers T.J. Houshmandzadeh and Chad Johnson, as well as running back Rudi Johnson.

Pro Bowl Selections

• Corey Dillon (RB)

Schedule

OPPONENT	SCORE	RECORD
W New England Patriots	23–17	1–0
W Baltimore Ravens	21–10	2–0
L @ San Diego Chargers	14–28	2–1
L @ Pittsburgh Steelers	7–16	2–2
W Cleveland Browns	24–14	3–2
L Chicago Bears	0–24	3–3
W @ Detroit Lions	31–27	4–3
L @ Jacksonville Jaguars	13–30	4–4
L Tennessee Titans	7–20	4–5
L @ Cleveland Browns	0–18	4–6
L Tampa Bay Buccaneers (OT)	13–16	4–7
L Jacksonville Jaguars	10–14	4–8
L @ New York Jets	14–15	4–9
L @ Baltimore Ravens	0–16	4–10
W Pittsburgh Steelers (OT)	26–23	5–10
W @ Tennessee Titans	23–21	6–10

Season Leaders

CATEGORY	TOTAL	PLAYER
Passing Yards	3,216	Jon Kitna
Rushing Yards	1,315	Corey Dillon
Receiving Yards	819	Darnay Scott
Receptions	70	Peter Warrick
Interceptions	3	A. Hawkins, K. Kaesviharn
Sacks	9	Reinard Wilson
Points	78	Corey Dillon

Key Additions:
T.J. Houshmandzadeh (draft), Chad Johnson (draft), Rudi Johnson (draft), Jon Kitna (free agent), Lorenzo Neal (free agent), Justin Smith (draft)

Takeo Spikes registered 100+ tackles in all five seasons with the Bengals.

Starting Lineup

OFFENSE	POSITION
Jon Kitna	QB
Corey Dillon	RB
Lorenzo Neal	RB
Darnay Scott	WR
Peter Warrick	WR
Tony McGee	TE
Richmond Webb	LT
Matt O'Dwyer	LG
Rich Braham	C
Mike Goff	RG
Willie Anderson	RT

DEFENSE	POSITION
Vaughn Booker	DE
Oliver Gibson	DT
Tony Williams	DT
Justin Smith	DE
Steve Foley	OLB
Brian Simmons	MLB
Takeo Spikes	OLB
Mark Roman	CB
Artrell Hawkins	CB
JoJuan Armour	SS
Cory Hall	FS

SPECIAL TEAMS	POSITION
Neil Rackers	K
Curtis Keaton	KR
Nick Harris	P
Peter Warrick	PR

2–14
Fourth in AFC North

The Bengals hit rock bottom in 2002, following the NFL's realignment of divisions. Cincinnati finished dead last in the AFC North with a 2–14 record—the fewest wins in team history—and received the top pick in the 2003 NFL Draft.

Cincinnati failed to score double-digit points in each of their first four games and averaged an abysmal 5.75 points per game over that span. Free agent quarterback Gus Frerotte started the first three games before former top pick Akili Smith got the nod in a 35–7 blowout loss to the Tampa Bay Buccaneers in Week 4.

The Bengals turned to Jon Kitna for the remainder of the season. He helped calm the waters, bringing some consistency to the quarterback position.

Cincinnati lost another three games but crushed the Houston Texans, 38–3, in Week 9. Kitna threw four touchdown passes, and Artrell Hawkins tied the franchise record with a 102-yard interception return for a touchdown in the road win.

The Bengals couldn't build on it, however, losing six more games before their next win. Of those six losses, three were one-possession games.

As bad as the 2002 Bengals were, they did show some potential. Second-year wide receiver Chad Johnson emerged as one of the best players on the team, hauling in 69 catches for 1,166 yards and five touchdowns. He topped the 100-yard receiving mark five times. Star running back Corey Dillon topped the 1,100-yard rushing mark for a sixth straight season, finishing with 1,311 yards and seven touchdowns. Fullback Lorenzo Neal led the way for Dillon and was the Bengals' lone Pro Bowl representative.

By the end of the 2002 campaign, it was clear that the franchise needed to move in a new direction. The Bengals fired head coach Dick LeBeau after the worst season in team history.

Pro Bowl Selections

- Lorenzo Neal (RB)

Schedule

OPPONENT	SCORE	RECORD
L San Diego Chargers	6–34	0–1
L @ Cleveland Browns	7–20	0–2
L @ Atlanta Falcons	3–30	0–3
L Tampa Bay Buccaneers	7–35	0–4
L @ Indianapolis Colts	21–28	0–5
L Pittsburgh Steelers	7–34	0–6
L Tennessee Titans	24–30	0–7
W @ Houston Texans	38–3	1–7
L @ Baltimore Ravens	27–38	1–8
L Cleveland Browns	20–27	1–9
L @ Pittsburgh Steelers	21–29	1–10
L Baltimore Ravens	23–27	1–11
L @ Carolina Panthers	31–52	1–12
L Jacksonville Jaguars	15–29	1–13
W New Orleans Saints	20–13	2–13
L @ Buffalo Bills	9–27	2–14

Season Leaders

CATEGORY	TOTAL	PLAYER
Passing Yards	3,178	Jon Kitna
Rushing Yards	1,311	Corey Dillon
Receiving Yards	1,166	Chad Johnson
Receptions	69	Chad Johnson
Interceptions	2	A. Hawkins, K. Kaesviharn
Sacks	6.5	Justin Smith
Points	75	Neil Rackers

Key Additions:
Levi Jones (draft)

Starting Lineup

OFFENSE	POSITION
Jon Kitna	QB
Corey Dillon	RB
Lorenzo Neal	RB
Chad Johnson	WR
Peter Warrick	WR
Matt Schobel	TE
Levi Jones	LT
Matt O'Dwyer	LG
Rich Braham	C
Mike Goff	RG
Willie Anderson	RT

DEFENSE	POSITION
Bernard Whittington	DE
Oliver Gibson	DT
Tony Williams	DT
Justin Smith	DE
Canute Curtis	OLB
Brian Simmons	MLB
Takeo Spikes	OLB
Jeff Burris	CB
Artrell Hawkins	CB
JoJuan Armour	SS
Cory Hall	FS

SPECIAL TEAMS	POSITION
Neil Rackers	K
Brandon Bennett	KR
Nick Harris	P
T.J. Houshmandzadeh	PR

In seven years with the Bengals, Justin Smith sacked the quarterback a total of 43.5 times.

8-8
Third in AFC North

Another new era of Bengals football officially began in 2003 when the organization completed a 15-day coaching search that ended with the hiring of Marvin Lewis. He became the ninth head coach in team history. Mike Brown hired the 44-year-old Lewis to turn around a franchise that had struggled for more than a decade. Lewis quickly added scouts to the NFL's smallest personnel department, and he brought renewed credibility to a franchise that desperately needed a face-lift.

On the field, the 2003 Bengals got off to a slow start. But Lewis's vision began to come together after the bye in Week 6. The Bengals beat the Ravens, 34–26, and then followed that with a 27–24 win over the Seattle Seahawks. After losing to Arizona in Week 9, Cincinnati rattled off four straight victories.

At 7–5, the Bengals had legitimate playoff aspirations. Veteran quarterback Jon Kitna was playing the best ball of his career, which allowed the staff to keep their top overall pick in the 2003 NFL Draft, Carson Palmer, on the bench. Palmer was able to sit and learn from Kitna.

In Week 15, Cincinnati scored 41 points against the San Francisco 49ers in a win at Paul Brown Stadium. During the game, flamboyant wide receiver Chad Johnson famously held up a sign after scoring a touchdown that read, "Dear NFL, please don't fine me again." (Johnson had been fined a number of times for everything from the shoes he wore to his touchdown celebrations.) Naturally, he was fined $10,000 by the league. The victory put the Bengals in a tie with Baltimore for first place in the AFC North.

That was Cincinnati's final win of the season. The Bengals lost to the Rams, 27–10, in Week 16 and fell to the Browns, 22–14, in the finale. Cincinnati didn't make the postseason, but Lewis had the team back on track for the first time in a decade.

Pro Bowl Selections

- Willie Anderson (OT)
- Chad Johnson (WR)

Schedule

OPPONENT	SCORE	RECORD
L Denver Broncos	10–30	0–1
L @ Oakland Raiders	20–23	0–2
L Pittsburgh Steelers	10–17	0–3
W @ Cleveland Browns	21–14	1–3
L @ Buffalo Bills (OT)	16–22	1–4
W Baltimore Ravens	34–26	2–4
W Seattle Seahawks	27–24	3–4
L @ Arizona Cardinals	14–17	3–5
W Houston Texans	34–27	4–5
W Kansas City Chiefs	24–19	5–5
W @ San Diego Chargers	34–27	6–5
W Pittsburgh Steelers	24–20	7–5
L @ Baltimore Ravens	13–31	7–6
W San Francisco 49ers	41–38	8–6
L @ Saint Louis Rams	10–27	8–7
L Cleveland Browns	14–22	8–8

Season Leaders

CATEGORY	TOTAL	PLAYER
Passing Yards	3,591	Jon Kitna
Rushing Yards	957	Rudi Johnson
Receiving Yards	1,355	Chad Johnson
Receptions	90	Chad Johnson
Interceptions	4	Tory James
Sacks	6	D. Clemons, J. Thornton
Points	106	Shayne Graham

Key Additions:
Shayne Graham (free agent), Tory James (free agent), Carson Palmer (draft), Eric Steinbach (draft), John Thornton (free agent)

Willie Anderson was named to his first of four straight Pro Bowls in 2003.

Starting Lineup

OFFENSE	POSITION
Jon Kitna	QB
Rudi Johnson	RB
Jeremi Johnson	RB
Chad Johnson	WR
Peter Warrick	WR
Reggie Kelly	TE
Levi Jones	LT
Eric Steinbach	LG
Rich Braham	C
Mike Goff	RG
Willie Anderson	RT

DEFENSE	POSITION
Duane Clemons	DE
John Thornton	DT
Tony Williams	DT
Justin Smith	DE
Adrian Ross	OLB
Kevin Hardy	MLB
Brian Simmons	OLB
Artrell Hawkins	CB
Tory James	CB
Rogers Beckett	SS
Mark Roman	FS

SPECIAL TEAMS	POSITION
Shayne Graham	K
Brandon Bennett	KR
Kyle Richardson	P
Peter Warrick	PR

8–8
Third in AFC North

After avoiding a losing season in 2003 for the first time in seven years, the Bengals hoped to take another step forward with the first overall pick of the 2003 draft under center: Carson Palmer was named the team's starting quarterback.

Palmer and the Bengals fell to 1–4 to begin the year. After splitting the next two games, Cincinnati went on a run. Led by Palmer, the Bengals posted a 4–1 record over that span, averaging 28.4 points per game.

The signature win of the season came on the road against the Baltimore Ravens. The Bengals trailed in the fourth quarter, 20–3. But Palmer found wide receiver Chad Johnson for two fourth-quarter touchdowns and connected with wide receiver T.J. Houshmandzadeh for a third score. Cincinnati tallied 24 fourth-quarter points to stun the Ravens, as Palmer led the Bengals to a 27–26 victory.

Not only did this stretch of games bring hope for the seasons to come, it also showed that Palmer and the Bengals were improving weekly.

Unfortunately, Palmer suffered a knee sprain in a 35–28 loss to the New England Patriots in Week 14. The second-year quarterback missed the final three games of the season.

Jon Kitna came in and played well, posting a 2–1 record over the final three weeks. Cincinnati finished at .500 with an 8–8 record for a second consecutive year.

The 2004 season proved to be Palmer's coming-of-age campaign. Since he hadn't played as a rookie, he experienced some early struggles. But the quarterback gave everyone a glimpse of what the future held for the Bengals—and fans were excited.

Right tackle Willie Anderson was an All-Pro for the first time in his career.

Schedule

	OPPONENT	SCORE	RECORD
L	@ New York Jets	24–31	0–1
W	Miami Dolphins	16–13	1–1
L	Baltimore Ravens	9–23	1–2
L	@ Pittsburgh Steelers	17–28	1–3
L	@ Cleveland Browns	17–34	1–4
W	Denver Broncos	23–10	2–4
L	@ Tennessee Titans	20–27	2–5
W	Dallas Cowboys	26–3	3–5
W	@ Washington	17–10	4–5
L	Pittsburgh Steelers	14–19	4–6
W	Cleveland Browns	58–48	5–6
W	@ Baltimore Ravens	27–26	6–6
L	@ New England Patriots	28–35	6–7
L	Buffalo Bills	17–33	6–8
W	New York Giants	23–22	7–8
W	@ Philadelphia Eagles	38–10	8–8

Season Leaders

CATEGORY	TOTAL	PLAYER
Passing Yards	2,897	Carson Palmer
Rushing Yards	1,454	Rudi Johnson
Receiving Yards	1,274	Chad Johnson
Receptions	95	Chad Johnson
Interceptions	8	Tory James
Sacks	8	Justin Smith
Points	122	Shayne Graham

Pro Bowl Selections

- Willie Anderson (OT)
- Tory James (CB)
- Chad Johnson (WR)
- Rudi Johnson (RB)

Key Additions:
Robert Geathers (draft), Deltha O'Neal (trade), Bobbie Williams (free agent)

Rudi Johnson rushed for more than 1,300 yards in 2004, 2005, and 2006.

Starting Lineup

OFFENSE	POSITION
Carson Palmer	QB
Rudi Johnson	RB
Chad Johnson	WR
T.J. Houshmandzadeh	WR
Tony Stewart	TE
Reggie Kelly	TE
Levi Jones	LT
Eric Steinbach	LG
Rich Braham	C
Bobbie Williams	RG
Willie Anderson	RT

DEFENSE	POSITION
Duane Clemons	DE
John Thornton	DT
Langston Moore	DT
Justin Smith	DE
Kevin Hardy	OLB
Landon Johnson	MLB
Brian Simmons	OLB
Deltha O'Neal	CB
Tory James	CB
Kim Herring	SS
Madieu Williams	FS

SPECIAL TEAMS	POSITION
Shayne Graham	K
Cliff Russell	KR
Kyle Larson	P
Keiwan Ratliff	PR

11–5
First in AFC North

At last, the Bengals awoke from their playoff slumber in 2005. Carson Palmer established himself as one of the NFL's best quarterbacks, and wide receiver Chad Johnson cemented his superstar status.

The Bengals finished 4–2 in the AFC North, winning their new division for the first time. They reached double-digit wins for the first time since 1988, and they had the makings of a Super Bowl contender. Up first, they hosted the Pittsburgh Steelers in the Wild Card Round.

Their Super Bowl dreams died on the Bengals' second offensive play of the postseason. Palmer completed a 66-yard pass to Chris Henry, but Steelers defensive tackle Kimo von Oelhoffen ran into Palmer's left knee after he made the throw. The star quarterback fell to the ground, writhing in pain. Palmer had suffered a torn left anterior cruciate ligament (ACL) and medial collateral ligament (MCL). The Steelers won the game, 31–17, and one of the most fun and exciting seasons in Bengals history came to an end.

Palmer's injury remains one of the biggest "What Ifs?" in team history. Many believed Cincinnati had the talent to make a deep playoff run and perhaps even win Super Bowl XL. (The Steelers added insult to injury when they defeated the Seattle Seahawks, 21–10, for their fifth Super Bowl title.)

Palmer threw a team-record 32 touchdowns and was selected to the Pro Bowl. Willie Anderson and Chad Johnson were both named first-team All-Pro. Johnson was undisputedly the biggest star on the team.

Rookie linebacker Odell Thurman proved to be another bright spot for the Bengals, tallying 105 tackles, five interceptions, and nine passes defended. Sadly, it was Thurman's only season in the NFL due to off-the-field issues.

Pro Bowl Selections

- Willie Anderson (OT)
- Shayne Graham (K)
- Chad Johnson (WR)
- Deltha O'Neal (CB)
- Carson Palmer (QB)

Schedule

	OPPONENT	SCORE	RECORD
W	@ Cleveland Browns	27–13	1–0
W	Minnesota Vikings	37–8	2–0
W	@ Chicago Bears	24–7	3–0
W	Houston Texans	16–10	4–0
L	@ Jacksonville Jaguars	20–23	4–1
W	@ Tennessee Titans	31–23	5–1
L	Pittsburgh Steelers	13–27	5–2
W	Green Bay Packers	21–14	6–2
W	@ Baltimore Ravens	21–9	7–2
L	Indianapolis Colts	37–45	7–3
W	Baltimore Ravens	42–29	8–3
W	@ Pittsburgh Steelers	38–31	9–3
W	Cleveland Browns	23–20	10–3
W	@ Detroit Lions	41–17	11–3
L	Buffalo Bills	27–37	11–4
L	@ Kansas City Chiefs	3–37	11–5
L	*Pittsburgh Steelers*	*17–31*	*0–1*

Season Leaders

CATEGORY	TOTAL	PLAYER
Passing Yards	3,836	Carson Palmer
Rushing Yards	1,458	Rudi Johnson
Receiving Yards	1,432	Chad Johnson
Receptions	97	Chad Johnson
Interceptions	10	Deltha O'Neal
Sacks	6	Justin Smith
Points	131	Shayne Graham

Key Additions:
Odell Thurman (draft)

Starting Lineup

OFFENSE	POSITION
Carson Palmer	QB
Rudi Johnson	RB
Jeremi Johnson	RB
Chad Johnson	WR
T.J. Houshmandzadeh	WR
Reggie Kelly	TE
Levi Jones	LT
Eric Steinbach	LG
Rich Braham	C
Bobbie Williams	RG
Willie Anderson	RT

DEFENSE	POSITION
Justin Smith	DE
Bryan Robinson	DT
John Thornton	DT
Robert Geathers	DE
Landon Johnson	OLB
Odell Thurman	MLB
Brian Simmons	OLB
Deltha O'Neal	CB
Tory James	CB
Ifeanyi Ohalete	SS
Kevin Kaesviharn	FS

SPECIAL TEAMS	POSITION
Shayne Graham	K
Tab Perry	KR
Kyle Larson	P
Keiwan Ratliff	PR

Carson Palmer (9) was protected by a stellar offensive line, which included Rich Braham (74).

Playoffs, at Last

The Bengals' infamous playoff drought started in 1991 and lasted much longer than anyone could've anticipated. Cincinnati missed the postseason for 14 consecutive years, posting a 71–153 mark. It was easily the worst stretch in franchise history; the team didn't have a winning record in any season during that span.

Finally, the streak ended in 2005 when Carson Palmer, Chad Johnson, Rudi Johnson, and the rest of the Bengals took the league by storm. Cincinnati started 4–0 and by Week 12 had already reached the eight-win mark, matching their highest total since 1990.

The Bengals then beat the Baltimore Ravens, Pittsburgh Steelers, and Cleveland Browns in consecutive weeks to improve to 10–3. They clinched their first-ever AFC North championship in Week 15 with a 41–17 road win over the Detroit Lions. The playoff drought was over, and fans had plenty of reasons to be excited about football again.

Cincinnati finished fourth in points scored and led the NFL in turnovers forced (44). An opportunistic defense, combined with a high-powered offense, made the Bengals one of the most dangerous teams in the NFL.

Yet the magical season came to a screeching halt in the Wild Card Round against the Steelers, when Palmer suffered a torn ACL and MCL on the second play from scrimmage. The Bengals still built a 10–0 lead in the first half but ultimately lost to Pittsburgh, 31–17.

It was an unfortunate end to a season that put the lost decade, the 1990s, to rest. This was a major accomplishment, even if the team didn't make a deep playoff run.

Without Pro Bowl quarterback Carson Palmer, the Bengals fell to Pittsburgh in the playoffs.

8–8
Second in AFC North

Despite undergoing knee surgery in January, Carson Palmer returned from his injury in time for the start of the 2006 season. He played well, and the Bengals put themselves in position to make another postseason run. Cincinnati began 3-0 with road wins against the Kansas City Chiefs and Pittsburgh Steelers.

With Palmer healthy and a young core around him, it looked like the Bengals were once again legitimate Super Bowl contenders. Instead, they lost five of their next six games, including a painful defeat at the hands of the San Diego Chargers. Cincinnati blew a 28-7 first-half lead and fell, 49-41. Chad Johnson gained 260 receiving yards in the loss.

The Bengals bounced back and looked primed to make the postseason for a second consecutive year, but they came up short in their final three games of the season. In Week 16, they suffered a heartbreaking loss in Denver. Palmer found wide receiver T.J. Houshmadzadeh for a 10-yard touchdown to cut Denver's lead to 24-23 with 41 seconds remaining. The Bengals were an extra point away from tying the game, but the snap on the try sailed wide of holder Kyle Larson, preventing Shayne Graham from even attempting the kick.

Special teams cost the Bengals again in Week 17. Cincinnati had to beat Pittsburgh and needed a Denver loss to get into the playoffs. Denver did lose, so the Bengals had their chance. With the game tied at 17 and just eight seconds remaining, Graham attempted a 39-yard field goal for the win. His kick missed wide right. The Steelers scored a touchdown just three plays into overtime, ending the Bengals' season with a 23-17 loss.

Willie Anderson was named first-team All-Pro for a third consecutive season. Chad Johnson joined him as an All-Pro for a second straight year.

Pro Bowl Selections

- Willie Anderson (OT)
- Chad Johnson (WR)
- Carson Palmer (QB)

Schedule

	OPPONENT	SCORE	RECORD
W	@ Kansas City Chiefs	23–10	1–0
W	Cleveland Browns	34–17	2–0
W	@ Pittsburgh Steelers	28–20	3–0
L	New England Patriots	13–38	3–1
L	@ Tampa Bay Buccaneers	13–14	3–2
W	Carolina Panthers	17–14	4–2
L	Atlanta Falcons	27–29	4–3
L	@ Baltimore Ravens	20–26	4–4
L	San Diego Chargers	41–49	4–5
W	@ New Orleans Saints	31–16	5–5
W	@ Cleveland Browns	30–0	6–5
W	Baltimore Ravens	13–7	7–5
W	Oakland Raiders	27–10	8–5
L	@ Indianapolis Colts	16–34	8–6
L	@ Denver Broncos	23–24	8–7
L	Pittsburgh Steelers (OT)	17–23	8–8

Season Leaders

CATEGORY	TOTAL	PLAYER
Passing Yards	4,035	Carson Palmer
Rushing Yards	1,309	Rudi Johnson
Receiving Yards	1,369	Chad Johnson
Receptions	90	T.J. Houshmandzadeh
Interceptions	6	Kevin Kaesviharn
Sacks	10.5	Robert Geathers
Points	115	Shayne Graham

Key Additions:
Johnathan Joseph (draft), Domata Peko (draft), Andrew Whitworth (draft)

Starting Lineup

OFFENSE	POSITION
Carson Palmer	QB
Rudi Johnson	RB
Jeremi Johnson	RB
Chad Johnson	WR
T.J. Houshmandzadeh	WR
Reggie Kelly	TE
Andrew Whitworth	LT
Eric Steinbach	LG
Eric Ghiaciuc	C
Bobbie Williams	RG
Willie Anderson	RT

DEFENSE	POSITION
Bryan Robinson	DE
Sam Adams	DT
John Thornton	DT
Justin Smith	DE
Rashad Jeanty	OLB
Brian Simmons	MLB
Landon Johnson	OLB
Johnathan Joseph	CB
Tory James	CB
Dexter Jackson	SS
Madieu Williams	FS

SPECIAL TEAMS	POSITION
Shayne Graham	K
Chris Perry	KR
Kyle Larson	P
Keiwan Ratliff	PR

In 2006, Chad Johnson led the entire league with 1,369 yards receiving.

2007

7–9
Third in AFC North

After just missing the playoffs in 2006, the Bengals brought back an offense that still had quarterback Carson Palmer and perhaps the league's best duo of wide receivers in Chad Johnson and T.J. Houshmandzadeh.

Cincinnati beat the Baltimore Ravens in the season opener on Monday Night Football, but things went into a tailspin after that. The Bengals lost four straight games, including a 51–45 loss to the Browns in Cleveland (a game that saw Palmer throw six touchdown passes) and a 24–21 loss to the Seattle Seahawks.

The Bengals improved in the second half of the season, posting a 5–3 record down the stretch. This included a win over the Ravens in which Shayne Graham scored every Bengals point, going seven-for-seven on field goal attempts. The team played their most complete game against the Tennessee Titans two weeks later. Chad Johnson caught 12 passes for 103 yards and scored three touchdowns to lead the Bengals to a 35–6 win.

Johnson had arguably the best season of his career, finishing with 93 receptions for a career-high 1,440 yards and eight touchdowns. He was named to the Pro Bowl for a fifth consecutive season. Houshmandzadeh set some personal records of his own. He nabbed 112 receptions, which tied for the most in the NFL. His 1,143 yards and 12 touchdowns were also career-highs, and he was named to his first Pro Bowl. Palmer threw for 4,131 yards, which set a new career-high at the time.

The 2007 season was head coach Marvin Lewis's first with a losing record for the Bengals. While the offense was better than average, the defense left plenty to be desired. They finished 24th in points allowed (24.1) and were dead last in total sacks (22). The Bengals fired defensive coordinator Chuck Bresnahan and linebackers coach Ricky Hunley after the season.

Pro Bowl Selections

- T.J. Houshmandzadeh (WR)
- Chad Johnson (WR)

Schedule

OPPONENT	SCORE	RECORD
W Baltimore Ravens	27–20	1–0
L @ Cleveland Browns	45–51	1–1
L @ Seattle Seahawks	21–24	1–2
L New England Patriots	13–34	1–3
L @ Kansas City Chiefs	20–27	1–4
W New York Jets	38–31	2–4
L Pittsburgh Steelers	13–24	2–5
L @ Buffalo Bills	21–33	2–6
W @ Baltimore Ravens	21–7	3–6
L Arizona Cardinals	27–35	3–7
W Tennessee Titans	35–6	4–7
L @ Pittsburgh Steelers	10–24	4–8
W Saint Louis Rams	19–10	5–8
L @ San Francisco 49ers	13–20	5–9
W Cleveland Browns	19–14	6–9
W @ Miami Dolphins	38–25	7–9

Season Leaders

CATEGORY	TOTAL	PLAYER
Passing Yards	4,131	Carson Palmer
Rushing Yards	763	Kenny Watson
Receiving Yards	1,440	Chad Johnson
Receptions	112	T.J. Houshmandzadeh
Interceptions	5	Leon Hall
Sacks	3.5	Robert Geathers
Points	130	Shayne Graham

Key Additions:
Leon Hall (draft),
Dhani Jones (free agent)

T.J. Houshmandzadeh led the NFL with 112 receptions in 2007.

Starting Lineup

OFFENSE	POSITION
Carson Palmer	QB
Rudi Johnson	RB
Jeremi Johnson	RB
Chad Johnson	WR
T.J. Houshmandzadeh	WR
Reggie Kelly	TE
Levi Jones	LT
Andrew Whitworth	LG
Eric Ghiaciuc	C
Bobbie Williams	RG
Stacy Andrews	RT

DEFENSE	POSITION
Robert Geathers	DE
Domata Peko	DT
John Thornton	DT
Justin Smith	DE
Rashad Jeanty	OLB
Landon Johnson	MLB
Dhani Jones	OLB
Deltha O'Neal	CB
Johnathan Joseph	CB
Dexter Jackson	SS
Madieu Williams	FS

SPECIAL TEAMS	POSITION
Shayne Graham	K
Glenn Holt	KR
Kyle Larson	P
Antonio Chatman	PR

4–11–1
Third in AFC North

The Bengals' 2008 season was one to forget. The team started 0–8, and star quarterback Carson Palmer only played in four games due to an elbow injury. Wide receiver Chad Johnson, the team's biggest star, missed three contests and played through a shoulder issue for most of the season.

Cincinnati picked up their first win in November, as reserve quarterback Ryan Fitzpatrick led the Bengals past the Jacksonville Jaguars, 21–19. The team tied the Philadelphia Eagles the following week and lost three more games, before finishing the season with three consecutive victories.

Wide receiver T.J. Houshmandzadeh played well, despite having depleted weapons around him. He finished with a team-leading 92 receptions for 904 yards and four touchdowns. It was Houshmandzadeh's eighth and final season in Cincinnati.

Running back Cedric Benson was another bright spot for the team. He signed with the Bengals after their Week 4 loss to the Browns. Benson ran for 747 yards and two touchdowns in 12 games. With former first-round draft pick Chris Perry not living up to expectations, Cincinnati needed to add talent in the backfield. Benson took advantage of the opportunity and helped fill a void.

Even with noteworthy years from Benson and Houshmandzadeh, the Bengals offense finished last in the league in total yards and in scoring. They never gained more than 350 yards and only surpassed 300 total yards in four games. Their highest point total of the season was 23 points, and they failed to reach the 20-point mark in 12 of their 16 games.

Given the injury to Palmer and with Johnson having his worst season since his rookie campaign, it's not surprising that the Bengals struggled. Still, plenty wondered if Marvin Lewis and this iteration of the team would be able to recapture the magic of their 2005 campaign.

This was the first time that Lewis failed to win at least seven games in a season, and it was the second year in a row that the Bengals finished with a losing record. The future of Cincinnati football looked bleak, despite three straight wins to end the year.

Schedule

OPPONENT	SCORE	RECORD
L @ Baltimore Ravens	10–17	0–1
L Tennessee Titans	7–24	0–2
L @ New York Giants (OT)	23–26	0–3
L Cleveland Browns	12–20	0–4
L @ Dallas Cowboys	22–31	0–5
L @ New York Jets	14–26	0–6
L Pittsburgh Steelers	10–38	0–7
L @ Houston Texans	6–35	0–8
W Jacksonville Jaguars	21–19	1–8
T Philadelphia Eagles (OT)	13–13	1–8–1
L @ Pittsburgh Steelers	10–27	1–9–1
L Baltimore Ravens	3–34	1–10–1
L @ Indianapolis Colts	3–35	1–11–1
W Washington	20–13	2–11–1
W @ Cleveland Browns	14–0	3–11–1
W Kansas City Chiefs	16–6	4–11–1

Season Leaders

CATEGORY	TOTAL	PLAYER
Passing Yards	1,905	Ryan Fitzpatrick
Rushing Yards	747	Cedric Benson
Receiving Yards	904	T.J. Houshmandzadeh
Receptions	92	T.J. Houshmandzadeh
Interceptions	3	Leon Hall
Sacks	3	Ndukwe, Odom, Thornton
Points	78	Shayne Graham

Key Additions:
Cedric Benson (free agent)

Starting Lineup

Chad Johnson WR   CB Leon Hall

Ben Utecht TE

Levi Jones LT   DE Antwan Odom

Cedric Benson RB

Andrew Whitworth LG   DT John Thornton   LB Brandon Johnson

Ryan Fitzpatrick QB   Eric Ghiaciuc C   SS Nedu Ndukwe

DT Domata Peko   LB Dhani Jones

Bobbie Williams RG   FS Marvin White

Stacy Andrews RT   DE Robert Geathers   LB Rashad Jeanty

Reggie Kelly TE

K Shayne Graham
KR Glenn Holt
P Kyle Larson
PR Antonio Chatman

T.J. Houshmandzadeh WR   CB Johnathan Joseph

Bengals Trivia

Marvin Lewis's total of 131 wins is more than double the wins of any other Bengals coach.

Pro Bowl Selections

- None

First NFL Tie in Team History

2008

2009

10–6
First in AFC North

The Bengals' 2009 season was a roller coaster of highs, lows, and tragedies. Cincinnati strived to rebound after an injury-riddled 2008 campaign. After suffering a heartbreaking last-second loss to the Denver Broncos in Week 1, the Bengals got a surprising lift from Antwan Odom. The defensive end, who never finished a season with more than eight sacks, took down Green Bay quarterback Aaron Rodgers five times in the Bengals' 31–24 win.

Cincinnati went on to start 9–3, and some thought they were legitimate Super Bowl contenders. Quarterback Carson Palmer was healthy, and wide receiver Chad Johnson was in the process of topping the 1,000-yard mark for the seventh time in his career. However, in Week 9, wide receiver Chris Henry suffered a season-ending broken forearm.

More than a month later, the unthinkable happened. Henry passed away on December 17, after falling off the back of a truck being driven by his fiancée. The tragedy was heartbreaking. Henry was only 26 years old. His wasn't the only death that occurred within the Bengals family during the season. Defensive coordinator Mike Zimmer's wife, Vikki, passed away unexpectedly on October 8, 2009.

Despite playing with heavy hearts, the Bengals held enough magic to bring home an AFC North championship with a Week 16 victory against the Kansas City Chiefs. Palmer found Johnson for a six-yard touchdown with 2:03 remaining to secure a 17–10 win and the team's first division title since 2005. Johnson held up a "1" and a "5" with his fingers to honor Henry after the game-winning score.

That's where the magic ran out. Cincinnati lost on the road to the New York Jets in the regular-season finale. They returned home to play the Jets again in the Wild Card Round of the playoffs. But the Jets beat the Bengals, 24–14, and ended Cincinnati's season.

Pro Bowl Selections

• Chad Johnson (WR)

Schedule

OPPONENT	SCORE	RECORD
L Denver Broncos	7–12	0–1
W @ Green Bay Packers	31–24	1–1
W Pittsburgh Steelers	23–20	2–1
W @ Cleveland Browns (OT)	23–20	3–1
W @ Baltimore Ravens	17–14	4–1
L Houston Texans	17–28	4–2
W Chicago Bears	45–10	5–2
W Baltimore Ravens	17–7	6–2
W @ Pittsburgh Steelers	18–12	7–2
L @ Oakland Raiders	17–20	7–3
W Cleveland Browns	16–7	8–3
W Detroit Lions	23–13	9–3
L @ Minnesota Vikings	10–30	9–4
L @ San Diego Chargers	24–27	9–5
W Kansas City Chiefs	17–10	10–5
L @ New York Jets	0–37	10–6
L *New York Jets*	*14–24*	*0–1*

Season Leaders

CATEGORY	TOTAL	PLAYER
Passing Yards	3,094	Carson Palmer
Rushing Yards	1,251	Cedric Benson
Receiving Yards	1,047	Chad Johnson
Receptions	72	Chad Johnson
Interceptions	6	L. Hall, J. Joseph
Sacks	8	Antwan Odom
Points	97	Shayne Graham

Key Additions:
Kevin Huber (draft), Rey Maualuga (draft)

Starting Lineup

OFFENSE	POSITION
Carson Palmer	QB
Cedric Benson	RB
Chad Johnson	WR
Laveranues Coles	WR
Daniel Coats	TE
J.P. Foschi	TE
Andrew Whitworth	LT
Nate Livings	LG
Kyle Cook	C
Bobbie Williams	RG
Dennis Roland	RT

DEFENSE	POSITION
Robert Geathers	DE
Domata Peko	DT
Tank Johnson	DT
Jonathan Fanene	DE
Rey Maualuga	OLB
Dhani Jones	MLB
Keith Rivers	OLB
Johnathan Joseph	CB
Leon Hall	CB
Nedu Ndukwe	SS
Chris Crocker	FS

SPECIAL TEAMS	POSITION
Shayne Graham	K
Andre Caldwell	KR
Kevin Huber	P
Quan Cosby	PR

In 2009, Robert Geathers (91) led the NFL in fumble-recovery yards with 113.

All-2000s Offense

QUARTERBACK: The Bengals finally left the dismal 1990s behind the moment they selected **Carson Palmer** (2004–2009) with the first pick in the 2003 NFL Draft. The USC product threw for 22,694 yards in 97 career games for the Bengals. His 154 touchdown passes rank fourth in team history.

RUNNING BACKS: **Corey Dillon** (2000–2003) and **Rudi Johnson** (2001–2007) outran the competition at running back. Dillon had three straight 1,300-yard rushing seasons from 2000 to 2002, and he set the NFL single-game rushing record when he gained 278 yards on the ground against the Denver Broncos in 2000. Johnson had back-to-back 1,400-yard seasons in 2004 and 2005. During the decade, he rushed for 5,742 yards, and his 49 touchdowns are good enough for ninth in team history.

WIDE RECEIVERS: The all-decade wide receivers are also easy choices. **Chad Johnson** (2001–2009) is the most accomplished wide-out in team history. He owns team records for total receptions (751), receiving yards (10,783), and touchdown catches (66). He was a six-time Pro Bowl player and was twice first-team All-Pro. **T.J. Houshmandzadeh** (2001–2008) led the NFL with 112 receptions in 2007 and topped the 900-yard receiving mark in five straight seasons. His 507 receptions are fourth in team history.

TIGHT END: Reggie Kelly (2003–2008) started 86 games. He didn't post huge numbers, but he was a quality blocker and brought consistency to the position for much of the decade.

TACKLES: The Bengals offensive line was stout for most of the 2000s. Some may be surprised that Andrew Whitworth isn't on the team, but **Levi Jones** (2002–2008) made 89 starts for the Bengals. Whitworth, on the other hand, switched between guard and tackle until the 2009 season. Right tackle **Willie Anderson** (2000–2007) was the undisputed standout of the unit. He ranked among the best offensive linemen in the NFL and was a first-team All-Pro in 2004, 2005, and 2006. Anderson is in the Bengals Ring of Honor. He allowed just 16 sacks in his entire career.

GUARDS: **Eric Steinbach** (2003–2006) spent four seasons with the Bengals after getting drafted in the second round in 2003. He started 62 games at left guard. **Bobbie Williams** (2004–2009) became the right guard after joining the team in 2004. He started 93 games in six seasons.

CENTER: **Rich Braham** (2000–2006) played both guard and tackle in the 1990s—and is a guard on our All-1990s team. He also started 82 games at center for the Bengals and makes this decade's team at a new position.

KICKER: **Shayne Graham** (2003–2009) made 86.8% of his field goal attempts—including 60 field goals in 62 tries from under 30 yards—and 98.8% of his extra points. He made the Pro Bowl in 2005.

KICK RETURNER: **Glenn Holt** (2006–2008) returned 122 kicks for 2,961 yards, including a 100-yard touchdown in 2007. He averaged 24.3 yards per return.

Statistics for the all-decade team are for the given decade only, unless otherwise noted.

All-2000s Defense

DEFENSIVE ENDS: Justin Smith (2001–2007) was productive throughout his Bengals tenure. He made 107 starts in seven seasons, finishing with 470 tackles, 43.5 sacks, and 28 quarterback hits. He had two interceptions and six forced fumbles. **Robert Geathers** (2004–2009) is our other defensive end. He appeared in 88 games and tallied 26.5 sacks, 52 quarterback hits, six forced fumbles, and four fumble recoveries. He intercepted two passes and returned one of them for a touchdown.

DEFENSIVE TACKLES: John Thornton (2003–2008) made 88 starts in six seasons with the Bengals, finishing with 235 tackles and 17 sacks. A run-stopping force in the middle, **Domata Peko** (2006–2009) played in 59 games and tallied 185 tackles, 4.5 sacks, and two forced fumbles.

LINEBACKERS: Takeo Spikes (2000–2002) and **Brian Simmons** (2000–2006) fill our two linebacker spots. Spikes started 47 games for Cincinnati, finishing with 350 tackles, 9.5 sacks, and 10 passes defended. He recovered eight fumbles, intercepted three passes, and scored two defensive touchdowns. Simmons had 534 tackles—including 35 tackles for loss—in 91 games. He added 17 sacks, 10 interceptions, six fumble recoveries, and scored three defensive touchdowns. Odell Thurman gets an honorable mention. He might've made a run at a spot if he had played for more than one season (2005).

CORNERBACKS: Our 2000s defense features three cornerbacks. **Johnathan Joseph** (2006–2010) was an underrated defender. He intercepted 14 passes and returned three for touchdowns over 67 games with the Bengals. **Tory James** (2003–2006) had 21 interceptions in four seasons. He also tallied 59 passes defended and 231 tackles over that span. He was named to the Pro Bowl

in 2004. Like James, **Deltha O'Neal** (2004–2007) spent four seasons in Cincinnati, including a 2005 Pro Bowl campaign. O'Neal led the NFL with 10 interceptions that season. He also had a game-clinching pick-six in a 2004 win over the Cleveland Browns.

SAFETIES: Nedu Ndukwe (2007–2009) had 198 tackles, five interceptions, and two fumble recoveries—both resulting in touchdowns—in 41 games. **Madieu Williams** (2004–2007) logged 290 tackles with 17 tackles for loss in 49 games. He intercepted nine passes and returned one for a touchdown.

PUNTER: Kyle Larson (2004–2008) appeared in 80 games and averaged 42 yards per punt.

PUNT RETURNER: Peter Warrick (2000–2003) was a dynamic player. His highlights included a 68-yard punt return for a touchdown in a win over the previously undefeated Kansas City Chiefs in 2003. (He also scored on a 77-yard reception in that game.) Warrick is the Bengals' punt returner of the decade, averaging 9.7 yards per return.

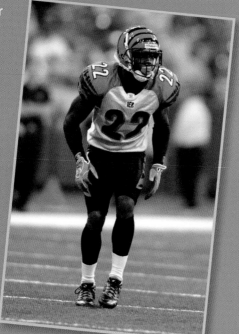

Johnathan Joseph was one of the league's top cornerbacks.

4–12
Fourth in AFC North

The Bengals' 2010 campaign may have been their most disappointing season in history. The team posted a 4–12 record and finished last in the AFC North just a year after winning 10 games and the division.

Ahead of the season, owner Mike Brown aggressively addressed the team's biggest weakness in free agency: depth at wide receiver. The Bengals signed former 1,000-yard receiver Antonio Bryant to a four-year contract. Instead of standing pat, the team went out and added Terrell Owens. The former All-Pro had a big personality, but the Bengals thought he could form a special duo on the opposite side of Chad "Ochocinco" Johnson. Suddenly, what had been a weakness appeared to be a strength. However, Bryant suffered a lingering knee issue and never played a snap for the team.

Fans had Super Bowl expectations for the first time since 2005. Many believed an offense led by quarterback Carson Palmer—and featuring running back Cedric Benson, along with Owens and Ochocinco—would be impossible to stop. Yet Cincinnati lost 10 straight games.

The Owens-and-Ocho experiment didn't work, and Palmer played one of the worst seasons of his NFL career. He completed 61.8% of his passes for 3,970 yards and 26 touchdowns but threw 20 interceptions. Palmer's struggles, combined with his roller-coaster season sent him and the franchise down a path of no return. The star quarterback demanded a trade following the season and even retired after the Bengals refused to deal him. Ultimately, the team traded him to the Oakland Raiders during the 2011 season for first- and second-round draft picks. Neither Owens nor Ocho ever played another down for the Bengals.

Brown retained head coach Marvin Lewis after voicing confidence in Lewis's ability to bring winning football back to Cincinnati.

Pro Bowl Selections

- None

Schedule

OPPONENT	SCORE	RECORD
L @ New England Patriots	24–38	0–1
W Baltimore Ravens	15–10	1–1
W @ Carolina Panthers	20–7	2–1
L @ Cleveland Browns	20–23	2–2
L Tampa Bay Buccaneers	21–24	2–3
L @ Atlanta Falcons	32–39	2–4
L Miami Dolphins	14–22	2–5
L Pittsburgh Steelers	21–27	2–6
L @ Indianapolis Colts	17–23	2–7
L Buffalo Bills	31–49	2–8
L @ New York Jets	10–26	2–9
L New Orleans Saints	30–34	2–10
L @ Pittsburgh Steelers	7–23	2–11
W Cleveland Browns	19–17	3–11
W San Diego Chargers	34–20	4–11
L Baltimore Ravens	7–13	4–12

Season Leaders

CATEGORY	TOTAL	PLAYER
Passing Yards	3,970	Carson Palmer
Rushing Yards	1,111	Cedric Benson
Receiving Yards	983	Terrell Owens
Receptions	72	Terrell Owens
Interceptions	4	Leon Hall
Sacks	9.5	Carlos Dunlap
Points	62	Mike Nugent

Key Additions:
Geno Atkins (draft), Carlos Dunlap (draft), Jermaine Gresham (draft), Adam Jones (free agent), Reggie Nelson (trade), Terrell Owens (free agent)

Starting Lineup

OFFENSE	POSITION
Carson Palmer	QB
Cedric Benson	RB
Chad Johnson	WR
Terrell Owens	WR
Jermaine Gresham	TE
Reggie Kelly	TE
Andrew Whitworth	LT
Nate Livings	LG
Kyle Cook	C
Bobbie Williams	RG
Dennis Roland	RT

DEFENSE	POSITION
Robert Geathers	DE
Domata Peko	DT
Pat Sims	DT
Michael Johnson	DE
Rey Maualuga	OLB
Dhani Jones	MLB
Keith Rivers	OLB
Johnathan Joseph	CB
Leon Hall	CB
Roy Williams	SS
Chris Crocker	FS

SPECIAL TEAMS	POSITION
Mike Nugent	K
Bernard Scott	KR
Kevin Huber	P
Quan Cosby	PR

Cedric Benson rushed for more than 1,000 yards in three of four seasons with the Bengals.

2011

9–7

Third in AFC North

If 2010 were the Bengals' most disappointing season, then 2011 was perhaps the most pleasantly surprising. Before the season began, franchise quarterback Carson Palmer said he would rather retire than play for the Bengals again; he was ultimately traded. In full rebuilding mode, Cincinnati also traded wide receiver Chad Johnson to the New England Patriots and chose not to re-sign wide receiver Terrell Owens. The Bengals were projected to be one of the worst teams in the NFL. After all, how could a team that went 4–12 the previous season be competitive without arguably the three most important offensive weapons?

It turned out these changes were exactly what the Bengals needed. They drafted wide receiver A.J. Green with the fourth pick in the 2011 NFL Draft and quarterback Andy Dalton in the second round (35th overall).

Those who thought the team would finish 0–16 (and some people did) were quickly proven wrong. The Bengals won their season opener in Cleveland. After jumping to a 13–0 lead behind their rookie quarterback, Cincinnati gave up 17 straight points. Dalton suffered a minor wrist injury and didn't finish the game. But a 41-yard fourth-quarter touchdown pass from backup quarterback Bruce Gradkowski to Green gave Cincinnati the lead again, and the Bengals eventually won, 27–17.

The Bengals went on to start the season 6–2. Dalton and Green had great chemistry, and Cedric Benson carried the load on the ground, running for 1,067 yards. It was his third straight season with at least 1,000 rushing yards. Defensive tackle Geno Atkins burst onto the scene with 7.5 sacks. Veterans like Chris Crocker, Thomas Howard, Manny Lawson, and Reggie Nelson played huge roles in defensive coordinator Mike Zimmer's defense.

Cincinnati cooled off in the second half of the season, posting a 3–5 record in the final eight games, but their 9–7 mark was enough to qualify for the postseason. They lost to the Houston Texans, 31–10, in the Wild Card Round, but the playoff loss didn't put a damper on what the team had accomplished. They were young and had plenty of talented assets. The Dalton-Green era had just begun, and their future promised to be bright.

Schedule

OPPONENT	SCORE	RECORD
W @ Cleveland Browns	27–17	1–0
L @ Denver Broncos	22–24	1–1
L San Francisco 49ers	8–13	1–2
W Buffalo Bills	23–20	2–2
W @ Jacksonville Jaguars	30–20	3–2
W Indianapolis Colts	27–17	4–2
W @ Seattle Seahawks	34–12	5–2
W @ Tennessee Titans	24–17	6–2
L Pittsburgh Steelers	17–24	6–3
L @ Baltimore Ravens	24–31	6–4
W Cleveland Browns	23–20	7–4
L @ Pittsburgh Steelers	7–35	7–5
L Houston Texans	19–20	7–6
W @ Saint Louis Rams	20–13	8–6
W Arizona Cardinals	23–16	9–6
L Baltimore Ravens	16–24	9–7
L *Houston Texans*	*10–31*	*0–1*

Season Leaders

CATEGORY	TOTAL	PLAYER
Passing Yards	3,398	Andy Dalton
Rushing Yards	1,067	Cedric Benson
Receiving Yards	1,057	A.J. Green
Receptions	65	A.J. Green
Interceptions	4	Reggie Nelson
Sacks	7.5	Geno Atkins
Points	132	Mike Nugent

Key Additions:

Clint Boling (draft), Andy Dalton (draft), A.J. Green (draft)

Starting Lineup

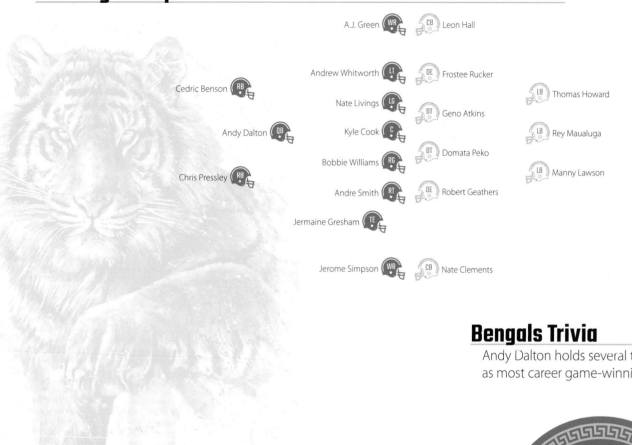

A.J. Green (WR)   (CB) Leon Hall

Andrew Whitworth (LT)   (DE) Frostee Rucker

Cedric Benson (RB)

Nate Livings (LG)   (DT) Geno Atkins

(LB) Thomas Howard

(SS) Chris Crocker

Andy Dalton (QB)

Kyle Cook (C)

(LB) Rey Maualuga

Bobbie Williams (RG)   (DT) Domata Peko

(FS) Reggie Nelson

Chris Pressley (RB)

Andre Smith (RT)   (DE) Robert Geathers

(LB) Manny Lawson

Jermaine Gresham (TE)

K Mike Nugent
KR Brandon Tate
P Kevin Huber
PR Brandon Tate

Jerome Simpson (WR)   (CB) Nate Clements

Bengals Trivia

Andy Dalton holds several team records, such as most career game-winning drives (24).

Pro Bowl Selections

- Geno Atkins (DT)
- Andy Dalton (QB)
- A.J. Green (WR)
- Jermaine Gresham (TE)

Dalton & Green:
Pro Bowl Rookies

2011

Best Catches

Few NFL teams can compare to the string of talent Cincinnati has enjoyed at one position in particular: wide receiver.

Isaac Curtis was the first legendary receiver to suit up for Cincinnati. He caught 416 passes for 7,101 yards and 53 touchdowns from 1973 to 1984. He passed the torch to Cris Collinsworth in 1981. The three-time Pro Bowl player finished with 417 receptions for 6,698 yards, spending all eight of his NFL seasons in Cincinnati (1981–1988).

"Downtown" Eddie Brown took the reins after the Bengals chose him with the 13th overall pick in the 1985 NFL Draft. He became the first player in franchise history to win NFL Offensive Rookie of the Year. Carl Pickens was named Offensive Rookie of the Year in 1992 and would go on to lead the NFL in receiving touchdowns (17) in 1995.

Chad Johnson made his mark just a few years after Pickens left the Bengals following the 1999 season. Johnson is still the Bengals' all-time leader in receptions (751), yards (10,783), and receiving touchdowns (66). He made six Pro Bowls between 2002 and 2010 and was twice an All-Pro. He led the NFL in receiving yards in 2006. Johnson is arguably the greatest receiver in team history. However, A.J. Green gives Johnson a run for his money, falling just short of Johnson in multiple receiving categories, including receptions (649), receiving yards (9,430), and receiving touchdowns (65). The seven-time Pro Bowl player helped Cincinnati make the playoffs in five consecutive seasons (2011–2015).

Ja'Marr Chase and Tee Higgins are the most recent wide receivers to make major impacts. They helped Cincinnati reach Super Bowl LVI. Chase became the third Bengals player ever to be named Offensive Rookie of the Year. He finished with 1,455 receiving yards in his first season—a modern-day NFL rookie record and the most receiving yards in Bengals history.

Drafted in 2021, Ja'Marr Chase became the newest in Cincinnati's stellar history of wide receivers.

10-6
Second in AFC North

The Bengals had shocked football fans everywhere when they made the playoffs in 2011. Andy Dalton, A.J. Green, and the rest of the team looked poised for an encore performance in 2012. Cincinnati started the year 3–1.

Their upward trajectory stalled when the Bengals lost four straight games for the first time since 2010. They fell to 3–5 on the year and were 1–3 in the AFC North.

Marvin Lewis's young team responded with a four-game winning streak that gave them the momentum they needed to make another playoff push. After a one-point loss to the Dallas Cowboys in Week 14, the Bengals won their final three games to finish 10–6 and earn a Wild Card spot. It was the first time the Bengals had qualified for the postseason in back-to-back years since 1981 and 1982.

Cincinnati traveled to Houston to play the Texans in the Wild Card Round for a second straight season. The Bengals played well on the road and were within striking distance late in the fourth quarter. Cincinnati faced third-and-11 from the Houston 36-yard line, trailing by six with 2:57 remaining.

Green beat his man and was open in the end zone, but Dalton overthrew him, and an opportunity was missed. The Bengals ultimately lost, 19–13. That play might have changed the trajectory of this era. It could have potentially snapped the Bengals' playoff-win drought and given Lewis his first postseason victory. Instead, Dalton threw the ball about two yards too far, and the Bengals lost the game.

Dalton and Green would go on to connect for plenty of touchdowns over the next six seasons, but the one they missed was bigger than any of the ones they hit.

Pro Bowl Selections

- Geno Atkins (DT)
- A.J. Green (WR)
- Jermaine Gresham (TE)
- Andrew Whitworth (OT)

Schedule

OPPONENT	SCORE	RECORD
L @ Baltimore Ravens	13–44	0–1
W Cleveland Browns	34–27	1–1
W @ Washington	38–31	2–1
W @ Jacksonville Jaguars	27–10	3–1
L Miami Dolphins	13–17	3–2
L @ Cleveland Browns	24–34	3–3
L Pittsburgh Steelers	17–24	3–4
L Denver Broncos	23–31	3–5
W New York Giants	31–13	4–5
W @ Kansas City Chiefs	28–6	5–5
W Oakland Raiders	34–10	6–5
W @ San Diego Chargers	20–13	7–5
L Dallas Cowboys	19–20	7–6
W @ Philadelphia Eagles	34–13	8–6
W @ Pittsburgh Steelers	13–10	9–6
W Baltimore Ravens	23–17	10–6
L *Houston Texans*	*13–19*	*0–1*

Season Leaders

CATEGORY	TOTAL	PLAYER
Passing Yards	3,669	Andy Dalton
Rushing Yards	1,094	Benjarvus Green-Ellis
Receiving Yards	1,350	A.J. Green
Receptions	97	A.J. Green
Interceptions	3	C. Crocker, R. Nelson
Sacks	12.5	Geno Atkins
Points	92	Mike Nugent

Key Additions:
Vontaze Burfict (UDFA), Terence Newman (free agent), Kevin Zeitler (draft)

Starting Lineup

OFFENSE	POSITION
Andy Dalton	QB
Benjarvus Green-Ellis	RB
Chris Pressley	RB
A.J. Green	WR
Armon Binns	WR
Jermaine Gresham	TE
Andrew Whitworth	LT
Clint Boling	LG
Jeff Faine	C
Kevin Zeitler	RG
Andre Smith	RT

DEFENSE	POSITION
Robert Geathers	DE
Domata Peko	DT
Geno Atkins	DT
Michael Johnson	DE
Manny Lawson	OLB
Rey Maualuga	MLB
Vontaze Burfict	OLB
Terence Newman	CB
Leon Hall	CB
Chris Crocker	SS
Reggie Nelson	FS

SPECIAL TEAMS	POSITION
Mike Nugent	K
Brandon Tate	KR
Kevin Huber	P
Adam Jones	PR

11-5
First in AFC North

The 2013 Bengals had two years of success to build upon. They set their sights upon winning the AFC North and making a playoff run.

They started the season 2–2, which included a wild game against the Green Bay Packers at Paul Brown Stadium. Star quarterback Aaron Rodgers led his Packers to a 30–14 lead, but Cincinnati showed signs of life when Andy Dalton connected downfield with A.J. Green for a 20-yard touchdown. Two Rodgers interceptions on Green Bay's next two possessions opened the door for the Bengals, and Dalton answered, hitting wide receiver Marvin Jones for an 11-yard score. The comeback was completed with four minutes left in the game. Safety Reggie Nelson forced a fumbled that was recovered by cornerback Terence Newman and returned 58 yards for what proved to be the game-winner. The Bengals pulled off the upset, 34–30.

Cincinnati used four-game and three-game winning streaks to propel themselves to their first division championship of the Andy Dalton era. That set the stage for what many thought would be the end of the postseason-victory drought. The Bengals hadn't won a playoff game in 22 years.

That was supposed to change on January 5, 2014, when they hosted the San Diego Chargers. The Chargers took a quick 7–0 lead, but Dalton answered with a second-quarter rally. Jermaine Gresham's four-yard touchdown tied the game. Rookie running back Giovani Bernard fumbled at the four-yard line late in the second quarter, which likely cost the Bengals a touchdown. But Mike Nugent added a field goal as time expired in the half to give Cincinnati a 10-7 lead. That was the last time the Bengals would score.

Midway through the third quarter, Dalton lost a fumble when Cincinnati was driving. He threw an interception on the following drive. The Chargers went on a 20–0 run in the second half, which included a 58-yard touchdown run by Ronnie Brown. The Bengals' season ended with a 27–10 defeat.

Pro Bowl Selections

- Vontaze Burfict (LB)
- A.J. Green (WR)

Schedule

OPPONENT	SCORE	RECORD
L @ Chicago Bears	21–24	0–1
W Pittsburgh Steelers	20–10	1–1
W Green Bay Packers	34–30	2–1
L @ Cleveland Browns	6–17	2–2
W New England Patriots	13–6	3–2
W @ Buffalo Bills (OT)	27–24	4–2
W @ Detroit Lions	27–24	5–2
W New York Jets	49–9	6–2
L @ Miami Dolphins (OT)	20–22	6–3
L @ Baltimore Ravens (OT)	17–20	6–4
W Cleveland Browns	41–20	7–4
W @ San Diego Chargers	17–10	8–4
W Indianapolis Colts	42–28	9–4
L @ Pittsburgh Steelers	20–30	9–5
W Minnesota Vikings	42–14	10–5
W Baltimore Ravens	34–17	11–5
L *San Diego Chargers*	*10–27*	*0–1*

Season Leaders

CATEGORY	TOTAL	PLAYER
Passing Yards	4,293	Andy Dalton
Rushing Yards	756	Benjarvus Green-Ellis
Receiving Yards	1,426	A.J. Green
Receptions	98	A.J. Green
Interceptions	3	A. Jones, D. Kirkpatrick
Sacks	7.5	C. Dunlap, W. Gilberry
Points	106	Mike Nugent

Key Additions:
Giovani Bernard (draft),
James Harrison (free agent)

Starting Lineup

OFFENSE	POSITION
Andy Dalton	QB
Benjarvus Green-Ellis	RB
A.J. Green	WR
Mohamed Sanu	WR
Tyler Eifert	TE
Jermaine Gresham	TE
Andrew Whitworth	LT
Clint Boling	LG
Kyle Cook	C
Kevin Zeitler	RG
Andre Smith	RT

DEFENSE	POSITION
Carlos Dunlap	DE
Domata Peko	DT
Geno Atkins	DT
Michael Johnson	DE
James Harrison	OLB
Rey Maualuga	MLB
Vontaze Burfict	OLB
Terence Newman	CB
Adam Jones	CB
George Iloka	SS
Reggie Nelson	FS

SPECIAL TEAMS	POSITION
Mike Nugent	K
Brandon Tate	KR
Kevin Huber	P
Brandon Tate	PR

Andy Dalton's 77 consecutive starts are the most ever by a Bengals quarterback.

10-5-1
Second in AFC North

The Bengals needed to get off to a good start in order to forget their disappointing end to the 2013 season. Most of the same faces were on the roster, including quarterback Andy Dalton and receivers A.J. Green and Marvin Jones.

Cincinnati began 3-0, which included a season-opening road win over the Baltimore Ravens. However, they were on the losing side of Bill Belichick's famous "On to Cincinnati" game: After a slow start to his team's season, the New England head coach said, "We're on to Cincinnati," in answer to doubts about his team and his aging superstar quarterback Tom Brady. The Patriots righted their ship against the Bengals in a 43-17 blowout and were ultimately crowned Super Bowl champions.

The Bengals dropped their next game and followed that with a tie. Then the injury bug bit. Green missed three games with a toe issue. Plus, Jones was already out for the entire season with an ankle injury.

The offense turned to rookie running back Jeremy Hill for a boost. The second-rounder answered with 929 yards rushing and six touchdowns in the final nine games of the season, averaging 5.4 yards per carry. The Bengals went 6-3 in that stretch and made the playoffs for a fourth consecutive season.

As injuries continued to mount, Cincinnati went on the road for a Wild Card matchup against star quarterback Andrew Luck and his Indianapolis Colts—a team that had beaten the Bengals, 27-0, earlier in the season. Green missed the postseason game with a concussion. Other key players, including Vontaze Burfict, Tyler Eifert, and Jermaine Gresham, were also out with injuries.

Luck and the Colts never trailed in their 26-10 victory. For the Bengals, it was a sixth straight playoff loss under Marvin Lewis.

Green topped the 1,000-yard receiving mark for a fourth straight year and made it to the Pro Bowl again. He joined legendary wide receiver Isaac Curtis as the only two players in team history to make the Pro Bowl in each of their first four seasons. Adam "Pacman" Jones won the league's kickoff-return title, averaging 31.3 yards per return.

Schedule

	OPPONENT	SCORE	RECORD
W	@ Baltimore Ravens	23–16	1–0
W	Atlanta Falcons	24–10	2–0
W	Tennessee Titans	33–7	3–0
L	@ New England Patriots	17–43	3–1
T	Carolina Panthers (OT)	37–37	3–1–1
L	@ Indianapolis Colts	0–27	3–2–1
W	Baltimore Ravens	27–24	4–2–1
W	Jacksonville Jaguars	33–23	5–2–1
L	Cleveland Browns	3–24	5–3–1
W	@ New Orleans Saints	27–10	6–3–1
W	@ Houston Texans	22–13	7–3–1
W	@ Tampa Bay Buccaneers	14–13	8–3–1
L	Pittsburgh Steelers	21–42	8–4–1
W	@ Cleveland Browns	30–0	9–4–1
W	Denver Broncos	37–28	10–4–1
L	@ Pittsburgh Steelers	17–27	10–5–1
L	*Indianapolis Colts*	*10–26*	*0–1*

Season Leaders

CATEGORY	TOTAL	PLAYER
Passing Yards	3,398	Andy Dalton
Rushing Yards	1,124	Jeremy Hill
Receiving Yards	1,041	A.J. Green
Receptions	69	A.J. Green
Interceptions	4	Reggie Nelson
Sacks	8	Carlos Dunlap
Points	117	Mike Nugent

Key Additions:
Jeremy Hill (draft)

Starting Lineup

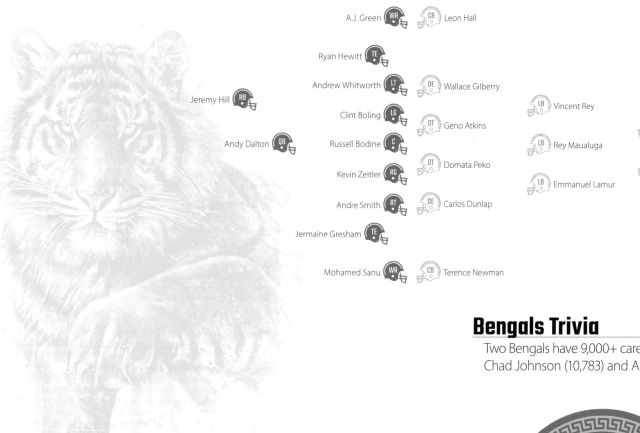

A.J. Green (WR)   (CB) Leon Hall

Ryan Hewitt (TE)

Andrew Whitworth (LT)   (DE) Wallace Gilberry

Jeremy Hill (RB)

Clint Boling (LG)   (DT) Geno Atkins

Andy Dalton (QB)   Russell Bodine (C)

Kevin Zeitler (RG)   (DT) Domata Peko

Andre Smith (RT)   (DE) Carlos Dunlap

Jermaine Gresham (TE)

Mohamed Sanu (WR)   (CB) Terence Newman

(LB) Vincent Rey

(SS) George Iloka

(LB) Rey Maualuga

(FS) Reggie Nelson

(LB) Emmanuel Lamur

K Mike Nugent
KR Adam Jones
P Kevin Huber
PR Adam Jones

Bengals Trivia

Two Bengals have 9,000+ career receiving yards: Chad Johnson (10,783) and A.J. Green (9,430).

Fourth Straight
Playoff Season

2014

Pro Bowl Selections

- Geno Atkins (DT)
- Andy Dalton (QB)
- A.J. Green (WR)
- Kevin Huber (P)

12–4
First in AFC North

The 2015 campaign was one of the best in franchise history. The Bengals started 8–0, becoming the first AFC North/Central team to post such a mark. Their eight straight wins also tied a franchise record. The streak included an improbable comeback over the Seattle Seahawks in Week 5. Cincinnati trailed, 24–7, entering the fourth quarter but scored 20 unanswered points to win.

Heading into a Week 14 matchup with the Pittsburgh Steelers, Cincinnati had a realistic chance of earning a top seed in the postseason, but quarterback Andy Dalton suffered a broken thumb while trying to make a tackle following an interception. He was having the best season of his career, but the injury sidelined him for the duration of it.

Reserve quarterback AJ McCarron played admirably, but Cincinnati fell to the third seed in the AFC playoffs. The Bengals hosted the Steelers in the Wild Card Round. Cincinnati trailed, 15–0, going into the fourth quarter, but they rallied to take a 16–15 lead with 1:50 remaining.

On Pittsburgh's next offensive play, linebacker Vontaze Burfict intercepted a pass to give Cincinnati the ball at the Steelers' 26-yard line—and a perfect opportunity to run out the clock. But an epic playoff meltdown cost the Bengals their first playoff win since the 1990 season. Running back Jeremy Hill fumbled, and the Steelers recovered, giving them one more chance.

Quarterback Ben Roethlisberger led his team into Bengals territory, but time was running out. Burfict was flagged for unnecessary roughness, and the 15-yard penalty put the Steelers in field goal range. Cornerback Adam "Pacman" Jones was then called for unsportsmanlike conduct. Those 30 yards of penalties led to a 35-yard field goal by Chris Boswell. The Bengals fell, 18–16, in the most heartbreaking loss of the Marvin Lewis era.

Pro Bowl Selections

- Geno Atkins (DT)
- Carlos Dunlap (DE)
- Tyler Eifert (TE)
- A.J. Green (WR)
- Adam Jones (CB)
- Reggie Nelson (S)
- Cedric Peerman (ST)
- Andrew Whitworth (OT)

Schedule

	OPPONENT	SCORE	RECORD
W	@ Oakland Raiders	33–13	1–0
W	San Diego Chargers	24–19	2–0
W	@ Baltimore Ravens	28–24	3–0
W	Kansas City Chiefs	36–21	4–0
W	Seattle Seahawks (OT)	27–24	5–0
W	@ Buffalo Bills	34–21	6–0
W	@ Pittsburgh Steelers	16–10	7–0
W	Cleveland Browns	31–10	8–0
L	Houston Texans	6–10	8–1
L	@ Arizona Cardinals	31–34	8–2
W	Saint Louis Rams	31–7	9–2
W	@ Cleveland Browns	37–3	10–2
L	Pittsburgh Steelers	20–33	10–3
W	@ San Francisco 49ers	24–14	11–3
L	@ Denver Broncos (OT)	17–20	11–4
W	Baltimore Ravens	24–16	12–4
L	*Pittsburgh Steelers*	*16–18*	*0–1*

Season Leaders

CATEGORY	TOTAL	PLAYER
Passing Yards	3,250	Andy Dalton
Rushing Yards	794	Jeremy Hill
Receiving Yards	1,297	A.J. Green
Receptions	86	A.J. Green
Interceptions	8	Reggie Nelson
Sacks	13.5	Carlos Dunlap
Points	117	Mike Nugent

Key Additions:
Michael Johnson (free agent)

A.J. Green made the Pro Bowl in each of his first seven NFL seasons.

Starting Lineup

OFFENSE	POSITION
Andy Dalton	QB
Jeremy Hill	RB
A.J. Green	WR
Marvin Jones	WR
Tyler Eifert	TE
Ryan Hewitt	TE
Andrew Whitworth	LT
Clint Boling	LG
Russell Bodine	C
Kevin Zeitler	RG
Andre Smith	RT

DEFENSE	POSITION
Carlos Dunlap	DE
Domata Peko	DT
Geno Atkins	DT
Michael Johnson	DE
A.J. Hawk	OLB
Rey Maualuga	MLB
Vontaze Burfict	OLB
Dre Kirkpatrick	CB
Adam Jones	CB
George Iloka	SS
Reggie Nelson	FS

SPECIAL TEAMS	POSITION
Mike Nugent	K
Brandon Tate	KR
Kevin Huber	P
Brandon Tate	PR

6-9-1
Third in AFC North

The Bengals felt like they could make another run in 2016, despite losing key pieces in free agency such as wide receivers Marvin Jones and Mohamed Sanu. In reality, the organization never seemed to recover from the playoff collapse in 2015. Cincinnati started 1–0. It was the first and last time they'd be above .500 during the 2016 campaign. Their offense was out of sync—but not for a lack of effort by A.J. Green. The star receiver was on pace for the best year of his career, hauling in 66 receptions for 964 yards and four touchdowns in the first nine games.

Cincinnati was 3–4–1 going into their Week 9 bye week. They had made runs in the second halves of seasons before. Why should 2016 be any different? Health was a big reason. The Bengals lost three straight games. In the middle of that stretch, Green suffered a torn hamstring against the Buffalo Bills. His loss helped to derail any chance of salvaging the season.

Cincinnati did win three of their final five games to finish 6–9–1, but they missed the playoffs for the first time since 2010. It marked the fourth time that the Bengals had finished a season with a losing record under head coach Marvin Lewis.

The defense held their own, finishing eighth in the league in points allowed (315). However, the offense finished 24th in points scored (325).

Pro Bowl left tackle Andrew Whitworth departed from the team in free agency after the season. He signed with the Los Angeles Rams, creating a major void on the Bengals' offensive line. Right guard Kevin Zeitler signed with the Browns, another unfortunate loss for the team.

The Bengals had been close to making a Super Bowl run in 2015, but the team looked much different just 14 months later.

Pro Bowl Selections

- Geno Atkins (DT)
- Andy Dalton (QB)
- Carlos Dunlap (DE)
- A.J. Green (WR)
- Andrew Whitworth (OT)

Schedule

	OPPONENT	SCORE	RECORD
W	@ New York Jets	23–22	1–0
L	@ Pittsburgh Steelers	16–24	1–1
L	Denver Broncos	17–29	1–2
W	Miami Dolphins	22–7	2–2
L	@ Dallas Cowboys	14–28	2–3
L	@ New England Patriots	17–35	2–4
W	Cleveland Browns	31–17	3–4
T	Washington (OT)	27–27	3–4–1
L	@ New York Giants	20–21	3–5–1
L	Buffalo Bills	12–16	3–6–1
L	@ Baltimore Ravens	14–19	3–7–1
W	Philadelphia Eagles	32–14	4–7–1
W	@ Cleveland Browns	23–10	5–7–1
L	Pittsburgh Steelers	20–24	5–8–1
L	@ Houston Texans	10–12	5–9–1
W	Baltimore Ravens	27–10	6–9–1

Season Leaders

CATEGORY	TOTAL	PLAYER
Passing Yards	4,206	Andy Dalton
Rushing Yards	839	Jeremy Hill
Receiving Yards	964	A.J. Green
Receptions	66	A.J. Green
Interceptions	3	Iloka, Kirkpatrick, Williams
Sacks	9	Geno Atkins
Points	92	Mike Nugent

Key Additions:
Tyler Boyd (draft)

Starting Lineup

OFFENSE	POSITION
Andy Dalton	QB
Jeremy Hill	RB
A.J. Green	WR
Brandon LaFell	WR
Ryan Hewitt	TE
Tyler Kroft	TE
Andrew Whitworth	LT
Clint Boling	LG
Russell Bodine	C
Kevin Zeitler	RG
Cedric Ogbuehi	RT

DEFENSE	POSITION
Carlos Dunlap	DE
Domata Peko	DT
Geno Atkins	DT
Michael Johnson	DE
Vincent Rey	OLB
Rey Maualuga	MLB
Vontaze Burfict	OLB
Dre Kirkpatrick	CB
Adam Jones	CB
Shawn Williams	SS
George Iloka	FS

SPECIAL TEAMS	POSITION
Mike Nugent	K
Alex Erickson	KR
Kevin Huber	P
Alex Erickson	PR

"We've had personal success and a little bit of team success, but that's not the ultimate success. The only way to get the ultimate success is to become a football team totally."

—Marvin Lewis

Geno Atkins was a Pro Bowl selection in eight of 11 NFL seasons.

7–9
Third in AFC North

The Bengals' 2017 season got off to an awful start, and the team never recovered. Cincinnati scored just nine points in their first two games. They lost to the Houston Texans, 13–9, on Thursday Night Football just four days after a season-opening loss to the Ravens, 20–0. The Bengals fired longtime quarterbacks coach Ken Zampese, who had been promoted to offensive coordinator prior to the 2016 season.

Cincinnati rallied from an 0–3 start to get to 3–4 after a Week 8 win against the Indianapolis Colts, but the Bengals never won more than two games in a row all season.

This team was hoping to recapture the magic of 2015 with some young, exciting new playmakers on offense, but their plan didn't work. First-round rookie wide receiver John Ross dealt with injuries and didn't catch a pass, and second-round running back Joe Mixon didn't have the impact that most were expecting him to make as a rookie.

After losing longtime left tackle Andrew Whitworth and guard Kevin Zeitler to free agency before the season, Cincinnati's offensive line struggled. Andy Dalton was sacked 39 times and completed less than 60% of his passes. Mixon averaged just 3.5 yards per carry.

The regular season's most talked about play was also the most tragic. In a Monday-night game against the Pittsburgh Steelers on December 4, Bengals receiver Josh Malone caught a pass over the middle from Dalton. In what appeared to be a routine play, Steelers linebacker Ryan Shazier charged forward to tackle Malone. However, after the play, Shazier could not get up. He suffered a spinal cord injury that left him paralyzed from the waist down. (Fortunately, Shazier was able to walk again several months later.)

Star wide receiver A.J. Green remained a bright spot for the Bengals. He finished the season with 75 receptions for 1,078 yards and eight touchdowns. He became the only wide receiver since the 1970 AFL-NFL merger to start his career with seven consecutive Pro Bowls.

Schedule

OPPONENT	SCORE	RECORD
L Baltimore Ravens	0–20	0–1
L Houston Texans	9–13	0–2
L @ Green Bay Packers (OT)	24–27	0–3
W @ Cleveland Browns	31–7	1–3
W Buffalo Bills	20–16	2–3
L @ Pittsburgh Steelers	14–29	2–4
W Indianapolis Colts	24–23	3–4
L @ Jacksonville Jaguars	7–23	3–5
L @ Tennessee Titans	20–24	3–6
W @ Denver Broncos	20–17	4–6
W Cleveland Browns	30–16	5–6
L Pittsburgh Steelers	20–23	5–7
L Chicago Bears	7–33	5–8
L @ Minnesota Vikings	7–34	5–9
W Detroit Lions	26–17	6–9
W @ Baltimore Ravens	31–27	7–9

Season Leaders

CATEGORY	TOTAL	PLAYER
Passing Yards	3,320	Andy Dalton
Rushing Yards	626	Joe Mixon
Receiving Yards	1,078	A.J. Green
Receptions	75	A.J. Green
Interceptions	2	Darqueze Dennard
Sacks	9	Geno Atkins
Points	85	Randy Bullock

Key Additions:
Andre Smith (free agent),
Joe Mixon (draft)

Starting Lineup

A.J. Green   Adam Jones

Josh Malone

Joe Mixon

Cedric Ogbuehi   Michael Johnson

Clint Boling Geno Atkins

Russell Bodine

Andy Dalton

Trey Hopkins

Andre Smith Carlos Dunlap

Tyler Kroft

Vontaze Burfict

Kevin Minter

Pat Sims

Nick Vigil

Shawn Williams

George Iloka

K   Randy Bullock
KR Alex Erickson
P   Kevin Huber
PR Alex Erickson

Brandon LaFell  Dre Kirkpatrick

Bengals Trivia

All-time sack leaders: Eddie Edwards (84.5), Carlos Dunlap (82.5), and Geno Atkins (75.5)

Pro Bowl Selections

- Geno Atkins (DT)
- A.J. Green (WR)
- Clark Harris (LS)

6–10
Fourth in AFC North

The 2018 season began with optimism but quickly turned to disappointment. After starting the year 4–1, Cincinnati lost nine of their final 11 games. The Bengals finished last in the AFC North for the first time since 2010.

The skid at the end of the season also marked the end of Marvin Lewis's 16-year run with Cincinnati. He helped turn the franchise around and ushered in an era of playoff football—but by the end of 2018, fans could only think about another losing season and 27 years without a playoff win.

The Bengals did get hit with a plethora of injuries throughout the season. Emerging tight end Tyler Eifert only appeared in four games. Star wide receiver A.J. Green was only on the field for nine games, and starting quarterback Andy Dalton missed six contests. All three played vital roles in the team's 4–1 start, but durability was a major issue for the 2018 Bengals.

Even first-round rookie Billy Price missed six games and struggled in his first NFL season. Evaluators viewed him as a plug-and-play center, but the Ohio State product didn't deliver.

Lewis's final win with the Bengals came against the Oakland Raiders in Week 14. Powered by Joe Mixon's running and with steady play from reserve quarterback Jeff Driskel, the Bengals jumped to a 17–0 lead in the first half. Behind three second-half field goals from kicker Daniel Carlson, the Raiders were able to close the gap to 23–16 in the fourth quarter. But Mixon sealed the win with a 15-yard touchdown run.

Ultimately, the 2018 season made it clear to owner Mike Brown and the entire organization that it was time to go in another direction. Lewis won a franchise-record 131 games and four AFC North crowns. He led Cincinnati to the postseason seven times, including five straight years between 2011 and 2015. Yet he was 0–7 in the playoffs, and he posted a losing record in each of his final three seasons with the Bengals.

Schedule

	OPPONENT	SCORE	RECORD
W	@ Indianapolis Colts	34–23	1–0
W	Baltimore Ravens	34–23	2–0
L	@ Carolina Panthers	21–31	2–1
W	@ Atlanta Falcons	37–36	3–1
W	Miami Dolphins	27–17	4–1
L	Pittsburgh Steelers	21–28	4–2
L	@ Kansas City Chiefs	10–45	4–3
W	Tampa Bay Buccaneers	37–34	5–3
L	New Orleans Saints	14–51	5–4
L	@ Baltimore Ravens	21–24	5–5
L	Cleveland Browns	20–35	5–6
L	Denver Broncos	10–24	5–7
L	@ Los Angeles Chargers	21–26	5–8
W	Oakland Raiders	30–16	6–8
L	@ Cleveland Browns	18–26	6–9
L	@ Pittsburgh Steelers	13–16	6–10

Season Leaders

CATEGORY	TOTAL	PLAYER
Passing Yards	2,566	Andy Dalton
Rushing Yards	1,168	Joe Mixon
Receiving Yards	1,028	Tyler Boyd
Receptions	76	Tyler Boyd
Interceptions	5	Shawn Williams
Sacks	10	Geno Atkins
Points	96	Randy Bullock

Pro Bowl Selections

- Geno Atkins (DT)

Key Additions:
Jessie Bates (draft), Sam Hubbard (draft)

In 2018, Joe Mixon averaged an impressive 4.9 yards per carry.

Starting Lineup

OFFENSE	POSITION
Andy Dalton	QB
Joe Mixon	RB
Tyler Boyd	WR
A.J. Green	WR
John Ross	WR
C.J. Uzomah	TE
Cordy Glenn	LT
Clint Boling	LG
Billy Price	C
Alex Redmond	RG
Bobby Hart	RT

DEFENSE	POSITION
Carlos Dunlap	DE
Andrew Billings	DT
Geno Atkins	DT
Michael Johnson	DE
Nick Vigil	OLB
Preston Brown	MLB
Vontaze Burfict	OLB
Dre Kirkpatrick	CB
William Jackson III	CB
Shawn Williams	SS
Jessie Bates III	FS

SPECIAL TEAMS	POSITION
Randy Bullock	K
Alex Erickson	KR
Kevin Huber	P
Alex Erickson	PR

Marvin Lewis

After posting a record of 55–137 from 1991 to 2002, the Bengals were desperate for a culture change. With failed picks like quarterbacks David Klingler and Akili Smith still haunting the franchise, Cincinnati needed new leadership. They found the perfect person for the job.

After 12 straight losing seasons, the Bengals hired Marvin Lewis in 2003. Lewis had helped the Ravens win Super Bowl XXXV as their defensive coordinator, and he was arguably the top head-coaching candidate available. The 44-year-old gave Cincinnati some much-needed credibility.

The Bengals went 8–8 in each of Lewis's first two seasons before winning the AFC North and making the playoffs in 2005. Coach Lewis would go on to lead Cincinnati to four division championships and seven playoff appearances during his 16 seasons with the team. He posted a 131–122–3 record, and his Bengals qualified for the postseason in five straight years from 2011 to 2015.

Lewis instilled a winning culture in Cincinnati that hadn't been in place when he arrived. He posted a 0–7 record in the playoffs, and while that mark is unfortunate, it doesn't change the impact he had on turning this franchise around. He is an important part of Bengals history.

Lewis won a franchise-record 131 regular-season games between 2003 and 2018. His .518 winning percentage is third in team history behind Forrest Gregg (.561) and Bill Johnson (.545), who coached the team for four years and three years, respectively.

2–14
Fourth in AFC North

The 2019 season was a transition year for the Bengals. Zac Taylor became the 10th head coach in franchise history on February 5, 2019. After serving as an assistant on the staff of the reigning NFC champions, the Los Angeles Rams, the 35-year-old impressed the Bengals front office. The team chose to roll with the young, offensive-minded candidate.

Taylor's first season went as poorly as anyone could have imagined. After losing a nail-biter to the Seattle Seahawks in Week 1, Cincinnati quickly established themselves as one of the worst teams in the league. They started 0–11, losing six one-score games. Taylor was growing into his new role as head coach, and that process included shuffling quarterback Andy Dalton in and out of the starting lineup in favor of rookie Ryan Finley.

The Bengals' first victory came in Week 13 against the New York Jets. Cincinnati won, 22–6, at Paul Brown Stadium. It gave fans a small amount of hope that the future would be better.

An already thin roster dealt with injuries to some of the team's best players throughout the season. The Bengals took left tackle Jonah Williams with the 11th overall pick in the 2019 NFL Draft, but the rookie missed the entire season after suffering a torn labrum in his left shoulder. Star wide receiver A.J. Green never played a snap after suffering an ankle injury at the start of training camp. Other starters, including wide receiver John Ross and cornerbacks Dre Kirkpatrick and Darqueze Dennard, missed extended time with injuries.

Cincinnati remained competitive for a team that won just twice, but they struggled to finish games. However, their issues in 2019 certainly helped their future. They landed the first pick in the 2020 NFL Draft. That pick would change the franchise. Of course, it didn't make losing in the moment any easier to take.

Cincinnati finished 2–14 for the second time in franchise history (2002). Defensive tackle Geno Atkins was the only player on the roster to get named to the Pro Bowl.

Schedule

OPPONENT	SCORE	RECORD
L @ Seattle Seahawks	20–21	0–1
L San Francisco 49ers	17–41	0–2
L @ Buffalo Bills	17–21	0–3
L @ Pittsburgh Steelers	3–27	0–4
L Arizona Cardinals	23–26	0–5
L @ Baltimore Ravens	17–23	0–6
L Jacksonville Jaguars	17–27	0–7
L @ Los Angeles Rams	10–24	0–8
L Baltimore Ravens	13–49	0–9
L @ Oakland Raiders	10–17	0–10
L Pittsburgh Steelers	10–16	0–11
W New York Jets	22–6	1–11
L @ Cleveland Browns	19–27	1–12
L New England Patriots	13–34	1–13
L @ Miami Dolphins (OT)	35–38	1–14
W Cleveland Browns	33–23	2–14

Season Leaders

CATEGORY	TOTAL	PLAYER
Passing Yards	3,494	Andy Dalton
Rushing Yards	1,137	Joe Mixon
Receiving Yards	1,046	Tyler Boyd
Receptions	90	Tyler Boyd
Interceptions	4	Darius Phillips
Sacks	9	Carlos Dunlap
Points	105	Randy Bullock

Key Additions:
Germaine Pratt (draft),
Jonah Williams (draft)

Starting Lineup

Tyler Boyd (WR)   (CB) William Jackson III

John Ross (WR)

Joe Mixon (RB)

Andre Smith (LT)   (DE) Sam Hubbard

Michael Jordan (LG)   (DT) Geno Atkins   (LB) Germaine Pratt   (SS) Shawn Williams

Trey Hopkins (C)   (NT) Andrew Billings

Andy Dalton (QB)

John Miller (RG)   (DT) Josh Tupou   (LB) Nick Vigil   (FS) Jessie Bates III

Bobby Hart (RT)   (DE) Carlos Dunlap

C.J. Uzomah (TE)

K   Randy Bullock
KR   Brandon Wilson
P   Kevin Huber
PR   Alex Erickson

Auden Tate (WR)   (CB) B.W. Webb

Bengals Trivia

The Bengals have drafted first overall four times in history: 1994, 1995, 2003, and 2020.

Pro Bowl Selections

- Geno Atkins (DT)

All-2010s Offense

QUARTERBACK: The Bengals made the playoffs in five straight seasons from 2011 to 2015, and **Andy Dalton** (2011–2019) was a key part of that run. Dalton has the most touchdown passes in Bengals history (204) and is second in team history with 31,594 passing yards. He also threw fewer interceptions (118) than Ken Anderson (160) and Boomer Esiason (131).

RUNNING BACK: Giovani Bernard (2013–2019) is perhaps a surprise selection since he wasn't a regular starter. Yet he compiled more than 5,700 all-purpose yards. As a dual threat, he gained more than 800 yards from scrimmage in four seasons. He narrowly edges out Joe Mixon for the running back spot, largely due to the amount of play during the decade.

WIDE RECEIVERS: A.J. Green (2011–2018) is second in team history in most receiving categories, including receptions (649), yards (9,430), and touchdowns (65). The Dalton-to-Green combination became one of the best NFL connections after both players were drafted in 2011. **Tyler Boyd** (2016–2019) had 242 catches for 2,902 yards and 15 touchdowns in the decade. He helped bridge the gap between the Dalton and Burrow eras. He also gained a reputation for making big plays late in games, including a 49-yard touchdown on fourth and 12 in the final seconds of a 2017 road win over the Ravens. **Marvin Jones** (2012–2015) was a game changer when healthy, hauling in 15 touchdowns in three seasons, including four scores against the Jets in 2013. He beats out Mohamed Sanu for the third wide receiver spot.

TIGHT END: Tyler Eifert (2013–2019) narrowly overtakes Jermaine Gresham to make the team. Despite dealing with injuries throughout his career, he made a huge impact when he was on the field, finishing with 2,152 receiving yards and 24 touchdowns in 59 games.

TACKLES: The offensive line was one of the best in the NFL during the team's playoff streak from 2011 to 2015. **Andrew Whitworth** (2011–2016) will be in the Bengals' Ring of Honor one day and perhaps in the hall of fame. He's the best left tackle in team history not named Anthony Munoz. **Andre Smith** (2010–2015) was a steady presence. No one else could rival him at right tackle.

GUARDS: Clint Boling (2011–2018) is one of the most underrated players of the decade. He held down the left guard position for eight seasons and even moved to tackle when the Bengals were in a pinch. **Kevin Zeitler** (2012–2016) was a force for five seasons at right guard, starting 71 games.

CENTER: Kyle Cook (2010–2013) gets the nod at center for starting the decade strong, before retiring after the 2013 campaign.

KICKER: Mike Nugent (2010–2016) beats out Randy Bullock at kicker after leading the team in points for seven straight seasons between 2010 and 2016.

KICK RETURNER: Brandon Tate (2011–2015) makes the team ahead of Alex Erickson in a close battle. Tate's 3,517 yards on kick returns was the most by a player during the decade. He averaged 24.3 yards per return.

Statistics for the all-decade team are for the given decade only, unless otherwise noted.

All-2010s Defense

DEFENSIVE ENDS: Carlos Dunlap (2010–2019) is one of the best pass rushers in Bengals history. He officially holds the team's all-time record for sacks with 82.5. (Eddie Edwards had 84.5 career sacks, but that was before sacks were officially counted.) Dunlap also holds the team record in quarterback hits with 227. He was named to two Pro Bowls. **Michael Johnson** (2010–2013, 2015–2018) racked up 37.5 sacks and 354 tackles in eight seasons with the Bengals, including a career-high 11.5 sacks in 2012.

DEFENSIVE TACKLES: The Bengals defense was led by **Geno Atkins** (2010–2019) for most of the decade. He became one of the premiere defensive tackles in the NFL. Atkins finished his career with 75.5 sacks, which ranks third in team history. He was named to eight Pro Bowls and was twice a first-team All-Pro. **Domata Peko** (2010–2016) made 112 starts during the decade. He posted 14 sacks and added 28 quarterback hits while clogging up the middle.

LINEBACKERS: **Vontaze Burfict** (2012–2018) joined the team as an undrafted free agent and became a Pro Bowl player in 2013. He unfortunately gained a reputation for making dirty hits, but he was undeniably a special talent. **Rey Maualuga** (2010–2016) takes the other linebacker spot. He played for the Bengals for seven seasons during the decade and was a solid player, tallying 521 tackles, seven interceptions, and three fumble recoveries.

CORNERBACKS: It feels more appropriate to start three cornerbacks on this team. **Leon Hall** (2010–2015), **Terence Newman** (2012–2014), and **Adam Jones** (2010–2017) all make the cut. Hall intercepted 12 passes and returned two for touchdowns. Newman and Jones signed with the Bengals in free agency. They both helped to stabilize a secondary that was in flux after Johnathan Joseph's departure following the 2010 season. Newman had five interceptions in 41 games with Cincinnati, along with a 58-yard touchdown on a fumble recovery that helped the Bengals beat the Packers in 2013. Jones had 12 interceptions along with five forced fumbles, six fumble recoveries, and two defensive touchdowns.

SAFETIES: **Reggie Nelson** (2010–2015) grabbed 23 interceptions in six seasons. He tied for the league lead with eight interceptions in 2015 and made the Pro Bowl that year. **Shawn Williams** (2013–2019) edges out George Iloka for the second safety spot. Williams appeared in 106 games and totaled 408 tackles and 12 interceptions.

PUNTER: Cincinnati native **Kevin Huber** (2010–2019) was the Bengals punter all decade long. His career average was 45.3 yards per attempt.

PUNT RETURNER: **Adam Jones** (2010–2017) also takes the punt returner spot. He averaged 11.3 yards per return, the best all-time in franchise history.

Carlos Dunlap recorded a career-high 13.5 sacks in 2015.

4–11–1
Fourth in AFC North

To no one's surprise, the Bengals drafted quarterback Joe Burrow with the first pick in the 2020 NFL Draft. He gave the franchise and the fan base a renewed hope that they could compete for championships in Cincinnati. The team moved on from Andy Dalton, releasing him shortly after drafting Burrow. In doing so, they handed the keys of the franchise to the top pick, reigning Heisman Trophy winner, and national champion.

Burrow was not allowed to enter team facilities until July due to the COVID-19 pandemic, but the rookie didn't miss a beat. He quickly established himself as one of the league's best young quarterbacks, but the team around him wasn't ready to consistently win. The Bengals lost their first two games by one possession before tying the Eagles in Week 3. They picked up their first win in Week 4 but struggled to protect the new franchise quarterback.

After starting the year 2–6–1, the Bengals were on their way to picking up a big road win over Washington. But instead of taking a step forward, their trip to the nation's capital became a nightmare. Burrow was hit in his left knee while planting to throw a deep pass to Tyler Boyd. The young quarterback fell to the ground, writhing in pain. He suffered a torn left ACL and MCL. Not only was he out for the rest of the season, he also lost plenty of valuable NFL snaps. Instead of competing for Offensive Rookie of the Year, he was stuck rehabbing his injured knee in hopes of coming back in time for the start of the 2021 season.

The Bengals' most impressive win came against the Pittsburgh Steelers on Monday Night Football. Cincinnati was a 14.5 point underdog going into the game, but running back Giovani Bernard scored two touchdowns to lead the home team to victory. Linebacker Vonn Bell made a key hit, knocking Steelers wide receiver JuJu Smith-Schuster to the ground and forcing a fumble. That set the tone for the rest of the game, and the Bengals came away victorious, 27–17.

Pro Bowl Selections

- None

Schedule

OPPONENT	SCORE	RECORD
L Los Angeles Chargers	13–16	0–1
L @ Cleveland Browns	30–35	0–2
T @ Philadelphia Eagles (OT)	23–23	0–2–1
W Jacksonville Jaguars	33–25	1–2–1
L @ Baltimore Ravens	3–27	1–3–1
L @ Indianapolis Colts	27–31	1–4–1
L Cleveland Browns	34–37	1–5–1
W Tennessee Titans	31–20	2–5–1
L @ Pittsburgh Steelers	10–36	2–6–1
L @ Washington	9–20	2–7–1
L New York Giants	17–19	2–8–1
L @ Miami Dolphins	7–19	2–9–1
L Dallas Cowboys	7–30	2–10–1
W Pittsburgh Steelers	27–17	3–10–1
W @ Houston Texans	37–31	4–10–1
L Baltimore Ravens	3–38	4–11–1

Season Leaders

CATEGORY	TOTAL	PLAYER
Passing Yards	2,688	Joe Burrow
Rushing Yards	428	Joe Mixon
Receiving Yards	908	Tee Higgins
Receptions	79	Tyler Boyd
Interceptions	3	Jessie Bates
Sacks	5.5	Carl Lawson
Points	87	Randy Bullock

Key Additions:
Vonn Bell (free agent), Joe Burrow (draft), Tee Higgins (draft), D.J. Reader (free agent), Logan Wilson (draft)

Starting Lineup

OFFENSE	POSITION
Joe Burrow	QB
Giovani Bernard	RB
Tee Higgins	WR
A.J. Green	WR
Tyler Boyd	WR
Drew Sample	TE
Jonah Williams	LT
Michael Jordan	LG
Trey Hopkins	C
Alex Redmond	RG
Bobby Hart	RT

DEFENSE	POSITION
Sam Hubbard	DE
Mike Daniels	DT
Christian Covington	DT
Carl Lawson	DE
Josh Bynes	LB
Germaine Pratt	LB
Darius Phillips	CB
William Jackson III	CB
Mackensie Alexander	CB
Vonn Bell	SS
Jessie Bates III	FS

SPECIAL TEAMS	POSITION
Randy Bullock	K
Brandon Wilson	KR
Kevin Huber	P
Alex Erickson	PR

A consistent performer, Tee Higgins gained 3,028 yards receiving in his first three seasons.

10-7
First in AFC North / AFC Champions

In 2021, the Bengals went on one of the most improbable runs in NFL history and ended their playoff drought in the process. Quarterback Joe Burrow was ready for the start of the season—which now included 17 regular-season games—despite undergoing knee surgery on December 2, 2020. The Bengals star helped Cincinnati get off to a 5–2 start.

Rookie wide receiver Ja'Marr Chase was a key reason why the Bengals turned things around so quickly. The fifth overall pick of the 2021 NFL Draft got off to one of the best starts in league history, compiling 35 catches for 754 yards and six touchdowns in his first seven career games.

Burrow put on a historic performance in Week 16, throwing for 525 yards and four touchdowns in a 41–21 rout of the Baltimore Ravens. A 34–31 comeback victory over the Kansas City Chiefs in Week 17 clinched the Bengals' first AFC North championship and first winning season since 2015. They were one of the NFL's biggest regular-season surprises, but that was just foreshadowing what would happen in the postseason.

The Bengals broke their 31-year streak without a playoff win by defeating the Las Vegas Raiders, 26–19, at Paul Brown Stadium in the Wild Card Round. Then they knocked out the Tennessee Titans on a walk-off field goal by Evan McPherson—the first road playoff win in team history. Finally, they traveled to Kansas City and took out the Super Bowl favorite in overtime to become AFC champions for the third time in team history. Unfortunately, they fell short in Super Bowl LVI, losing to the Rams, 23–20. (See page 146.) But it was clear that a new era of Cincinnati football was here.

Burrow won the NFL's Comeback Player of the Year Award. Chase finished with a franchise-record 1,455 receiving yards and was named NFL Offensive Rookie of the Year.

Pro Bowl Selections

- Ja'Marr Chase (WR)
- Trey Hendrickson (DE)
- Joe Mixon (RB)

Schedule

	OPPONENT	SCORE	RECORD
W	Minnesota Vikings (OT)	27–24	1–0
L	@ Chicago Bears	17–20	1–1
W	@ Pittsburgh Steelers	24–10	2–1
W	Jacksonville Jaguars	24–21	3–1
L	Green Bay Packers (OT)	22–25	3–2
W	@ Detroit Lions	34–11	4–2
W	@ Baltimore Ravens	41–17	5–2
L	@ New York Jets	31–34	5–3
L	Cleveland Browns	16–41	5–4
W	@ Las Vegas Raiders	32–13	6–4
W	Pittsburgh Steelers	41–10	7–4
L	Los Angeles Chargers	22–41	7–5
L	San Francisco 49ers (OT)	23–26	7–6
W	@ Denver Broncos	15–10	8–6
W	Baltimore Ravens	41–21	9–6
W	Kansas City Chiefs	34–31	10–6
L	Cleveland Browns	16–21	10–7
W	*Las Vegas Raiders*	*26–19*	*1–0*
W	*@ Tennessee Titans*	*19–16*	*2–0*
W	*@ Kansas City Chiefs (OT)*	*27–24*	*3–0*
L	*Los Angeles Rams* (Los Angeles, CA)	*20–23*	*3–1*

Season Leaders

CATEGORY	TOTAL	PLAYER
Passing Yards	4,611	Joe Burrow
Rushing Yards	1,205	Joe Mixon
Receiving Yards	1,455	Ja'Marr Chase
Receptions	81	Ja'Marr Chase
Interceptions	4	Logan Wilson
Sacks	14	Trey Hendrickson
Points	130	Evan McPherson

Key Additions:
Chidobe Awuzie (free agent), Ja'Marr Chase (draft), Trey Hendrickson (free agent), Mike Hilton (free agent)

Starting Lineup

OFFENSE	POSITION
Joe Burrow	QB
Joe Mixon	RB
Tee Higgins	WR
Ja'Marr Chase	WR
Tyler Boyd	WR
C.J. Uzomah	TE
Jonah Williams	LT
Quinton Spain	LG
Trey Hopkins	C
Hakeem Adeniji	RG
Riley Reiff	RT

DEFENSE	POSITION
Sam Hubbard	DE
Larry Ogunjobi	DT
D.J. Reader	DT
Trey Hendrickson	DE
Logan Wilson	LB
Germaine Pratt	LB
Eli Apple	CB
Chidobe Awuzie	CB
Mike Hilton	CB
Vonn Bell	SS
Jessie Bates III	FS

SPECIAL TEAMS	POSITION
Evan McPherson	K
Brandon Wilson	KR
Kevin Huber	P
Darius Phillips	PR

"Guys who aren't going to be brought down on first contact, they'll get you fired up. When you see guys spinning away and getting extra yards, it fires you up."

—Zac Taylor

Logan Wilson had 100 tackles in his first season as a starter.

AFC Champions

Entering the 2021 season, star quarterback Joe Burrow was coming back from knee reconstruction surgery. Burrow was on the field for the start of training camp, and he was able to return to action for the start of the 2021 season.

The Bengals surprised everyone—nearly matching their combined win total from the past two seasons in the first seven weeks, going 5–2. They also won three straight games beginning in mid-December, including a 34–31 victory over the powerful Kansas City Chiefs to win the AFC North for the first time since 2015.

The magic continued in the postseason. Germaine Pratt intercepted Derek Carr's pass in the closing seconds of Cincinnati's 26–19 win over Las Vegas—their first playoff victory in 31 years. Burrow and the Bengals continued their run, beating Tennessee in the Divisional Round on a last-second field goal.

It looked as if the magic would run out in the AFC Championship Game. Cincinnati trailed the Chiefs, 21–3, late in the second quarter. But the Bengals scored 21 straight points, and kicker Evan McPherson delivered again, booting the game-winning field goal in overtime to give Cincinnati a 27–24 victory.

The Bengals came up just short in Super Bowl LVI, falling to the Los Angeles Rams, 23–20. Cincinnati held a 20–13 lead in the third quarter, but their offense stalled, and the Rams scored the game's final 10 points.

The Bengals won an AFC championship for the third time in team history. Along the way, they also won their first ever road playoff game.

Joe Burrow faced plenty of pressure during the Super Bowl. He was sacked seven times.

12–4
First in AFC North

The Cincinnati Bengals broke multiple franchise records in 2022. A year after their surprising run to the Super Bowl, Cincinnati established themselves as an elite team. The Bengals won the AFC North for a second consecutive season for the first time in franchise history. Quarterback Joe Burrow led the way, throwing for a franchise-record 35 touchdowns, despite undergoing an emergency appendectomy at the start of training camp.

Cincinnati went undefeated in November and December, closing out the regular season on an eight-game winning streak. The stretch started with a 42–21 win over the Carolina Panthers in Week 9. Running back Joe Mixon had his best game, rushing for 153 yards and four touchdowns. He also caught four receptions for 58 yards and added another score. His five touchdowns in one game set a franchise record. Of course, fans will never forget the game that never happened: A Week 17 matchup against the Buffalo Bills was canceled after Bills safety Damar Hamlin suffered a cardiac arrest during the game. Hamlin eventually made a full recovery.

The Bengals beat the Baltimore Ravens in the Wild Card Round of the playoffs, thanks to the "Fumble in the Jungle:" a game-changing 98-yard fumble return for a touchdown by defensive end Sam Hubbard. Next, Cincinnati took down the Bills in Buffalo. The team came up short in an AFC championship rematch from the prior season. This time, they lost to the Kansas City Chiefs, 23–20, on a last-second field goal by Harrison Butker. Cincinnati didn't win a Super Bowl, but they advanced in the playoffs in back-to-back seasons for the first time in franchise history.

Ja'Marr Chase led the team in receiving, finishing with 87 receptions for 1,046 yards and nine touchdowns in 12 games. Tee Higgins wasn't far behind, compiling 74 receptions for 1,029 yards and seven touchdowns.

Pro Bowl Selections

- Joe Burrow (QB)
- Ja'Marr Chase (WR)
- Trey Hendrickson (DE)

Schedule

	OPPONENT	SCORE	RECORD
L	Pittsburgh Steelers (OT)	20–23	0–1
L	@ Dallas Cowboys	17–20	0–2
W	@ New York Jets	27–12	1–2
W	Miami Dolphins	27–15	2–2
L	@ Baltimore Ravens	17–19	2–3
W	@ New Orleans Saints	30–26	3–3
W	Atlanta Falcons	35–17	4–3
L	@ Cleveland Browns	13–32	4–4
W	Carolina Panthers	42–21	5–4
W	@ Pittsburgh Steelers	37–30	6–4
W	@ Tennessee Titans	20–16	7–4
W	Kansas City Chiefs	27–24	8–4
W	Cleveland Browns	23–10	9–4
W	@ Tampa Bay Buccaneers	34–23	10–4
W	@ New England Patriots	22–18	11–4
	Buffalo Bills (Canceled)		
W	Baltimore Ravens	27–16	12–4
W	*Baltimore Ravens*	*24–17*	*1–0*
W	*@ Buffalo Bills*	*27–10*	*2–0*
L	*@ Kansas City Chiefs*	*20–23*	*2–1*

Season Leaders

CATEGORY	TOTAL	PLAYER
Passing Yards	4,475	Joe Burrow
Rushing Yards	814	Joe Mixon
Receiving Yards	1,046	Ja'Marr Chase
Receptions	87	Ja'Marr Chase
Interceptions	4	Jessie Bates, Vonn Bell
Sacks	8	Trey Hendrickson
Points	112	Evan McPherson

Key Additions:
Alex Cappa (free agent), La'el Collins (free agent), Ted Karras (free agent)

Trey Hendrickson was named to the Pro Bowl in 2021 and 2022.

Starting Lineup

OFFENSE	POSITION
Joe Burrow	QB
Joe Mixon	RB
Tee Higgins	WR
Ja'Marr Chase	WR
Tyler Boyd	WR
Hayden Hurst	TE
Jonah Williams	LT
Cordell Volson	LG
Ted Karras	C
Alex Cappa	RG
La'el Collins	RT

DEFENSE	POSITION
Sam Hubbard	DE
B.J. Hill	DT
D.J. Reader	DT
Trey Hendrickson	DE
Logan Wilson	LB
Germaine Pratt	LB
Eli Apple	CB
Chidobe Awuzie	CB
Cam Taylor-Britt	CB
Vonn Bell	SS
Jessie Bates III	FS

SPECIAL TEAMS	POSITION
Evan McPherson	K
Trayveon Williams	KR
Drue Chrisman	P
Trent Taylor	PR

PHOTO CREDITS

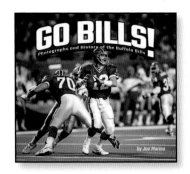

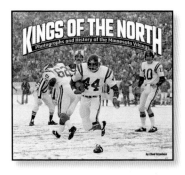

COLLECT THE FAVORITE FOOTBALL TEAMS SERIES